HOME WHERE I BELONG

"A new man."
(B. J. Thomas portrait by Chris Swallow)

B. J. Thomas

HOME WHERE I BELONG

as told to
JERRY B. JENKINS

WORD BOOKS

PUBLISHER
WACO, TEXAS

First Printing, October 1978
Second Printing, February 1979
Third Printing, June 1979
First Paperback Printing, April 1980

HOME WHERE I BELONG
Copyright © 1978 by Word, Incorporated
4800 W. Waco Drive, Waco, Texas 76703

ISBN 0–8499–2905–9
Library of Congress catalog card number: 78–59461
Printed in the United States of America

To my wife Gloria
and our daughter Paige
with eternal thanks
for their prayers
for my salvation

B. J. T.

And to my brother Jay—
may he be as conscientious
about his music

J. B. J.

"Y'know, I wish this book could have had more lightness and high points and comical relief, but we might as well face it: we're talking about what needs to be talked about, and this is no magical mystery tour."

—B. J. Thomas to Jerry Jenkins,
June, 1978

contents

preface

Pop singer B. J. Thomas, his wife Gloria, business manager Don Perry, and a few musicians had been waiting in a Nashville recording studio for an hour or so one frigid winter night late last year for Chips Moman to arrive.

Moman is not big; he looks more like a grown-up fourth-grade class cutup than a middle-aged man. This night his reddish beard and hair is topped by a faded denim cap and he's rubbing his hands as if they will never thaw

—the sub-zero weather a rude surprise to Nashvillians, even in the dead of winter.

It's hard to believe this freckle-faced leprechaun, impish and squinty-eyed, is regarded by those in the business as a genius in producing popular music. He sheds a leather jacket too light for the night, revealing a little pot belly under a yellow shirt inscribed: ARIZONA STATE MENTAL HOSPITAL / OUTGOING PATIENT. It's good for a new laugh with every handshake around the control room.

This is his bailiwick. He's written hundreds of hit songs, including many award winners, but his real love is the big board—the master control center in the recording studio where he flips switches, adjusts volume, mixes tracks, and runs the show.

Musicians can run through a song and think every-thing's gone perfectly, only to be stopped with three beats to go by Chips cutting in with, "Let's do it again." No one argues.

"If it don't sound right to Chips," says B. J. in his bass drawl, "then it ain't right."

By now the tiny, dimly lit room is crowded with a dozen people who have to duck gigantic speakers to sit in overstuffed couches and chairs. Through the soundproof window they can see the studio with its carpet-covered booths for singers and musicians. Illuminated only by multi-colored stage lights, the decor is contemporary haunted house, leaving everyone with shadowy visages and dreamy faraway looks. A chartreuse stuffed toy vulture—shoulders hunched as vultures will do—hangs its head over the top of the booth where B. J. will shortly record with his incredible range.

B. J. is wearing his unshaven studio face, a pullover sweater, blue jeans, and cowboy boots. Except for the unmistakable features and black hair, he could pass for a local college kid. His boyish face and clear eyes hide his thirty-five years, including a decade of slow suicide with drugs.

B. J.'s is the only name a majority of the public will recognize on this album, but at this stage of the production, Chips is every bit as important. He runs the session to give himself the best possible elements to work with later in producing the most marketable product for MCA records. After all the tracks have been cut and the vocal performances have been added (the purpose of this session), Chips can make or break the album.

"He's one of the few producers who can work well with B. J.," says Gloria Thomas, characteristically emphasizing the *B*. "There is just a minute difference between B. J.'s singing, singing good, and singing great. Chips knows and can keep him working until he's singing great. B. J. understands and appreciates it."

Not long enough ago to make the memory less abrasive, Chips Moman and B. J. Thomas were at each other's throats in this same studio. The singer of seven gold records and seller of nearly 35 million was strung out on marijuana, speed, and cocaine. The producer, a perfectionist but no saint himself, had run out of patience with a singer he couldn't respect.

They had tolerated each other until an ugly scene erupted. No one dreamed that Moman and Thomas would ever work together on an album again.

But here they were, a little more than two years later, and everyone on the scene—Chips included—was aware that something had changed. "You're different, man," Chips said more than once. Privately, B. J. told him of his new faith in Christ and why, months earlier, he had called Chips to apologize for past violence.

There were none of the old frustrations, cold wars, shouts, threats; things went so smoothly it was eerie. Some albums take weeks to cut. But for this one, after only a few days, seven songs had been completed and three or four more were nearly done.

When B. J. was in the booth, doing vocal performances with the instrumental tracks from the night before piped into his earphones, Chips played the control board like a piano, staring intently into space, then adjusting a switch here, a dial there. And when the lanky Texan singer hit notes and phrases just right, Chips would gaze heavenward with a grin.

B. J., of course, couldn't hear Chips rave: "Can't that boy sing!" At the end of each performance B. J. would wait at the microphone, his back to the control room, waiting for some word from Chips: Come in and listen, or Do it again. After a superb vocal on Chips' own "Blues River," the composer/producer was ecstatic.

"You're listening to one of the greatest singers in the

world," he exulted to no one in particular. "He sounds different than anybody ever has."

Patching in to B. J.'s earphones, he said, "Put the chairs on the wagon, son; the meetin's over!"

In reality, of course, for the singer of such monster hits as "Raindrops Keep Fallin' on My Head" and "(Hey Won't You Play) Another Somebody Done Somebody Wrong Song," the meetin' has just begun. The story of his escape from sin and death and the salvaging of a ravaged marriage is what this book is all about.

JERRY B. JENKINS

February, 1978
Deerfield, Illinois

1   the wakeup call

If only I had let my brother Jerry handle it.

He's been my road manager off and on—mostly on—for as long as I've been in the business. When we checked into the Loew's Mid-town Motor Inn on Eighth Avenue in New York that July night in 1968, we should have known trouble was brewing.

The black desk clerk didn't take kindly to a couple of slow-talkin' white dudes from the South, Martin Luther King Jr.'s death having been so recent and all. (You don't escape racial tension just by heading north, whether you're prejudiced or not—which we weren't.) Anyway, Jerry got into some kind of an argument with him right away, insisting that he didn't have to be so hostile.

The clerk got back at us the next morning when he "forgot" our wakeup call. Our morning engagements weren't that crucial the first day in town, but Jerry was furious. He grabbed the phone to give the clerk what for, but it was disconnected.

We decided to let it slide, but the next night Jerry thought he'd better make sure the guy had our phone plugged in and had us down for a wakeup call. I was scheduled for the Merv Griffin Show and was nervous enough without having to worry about getting up on time.

When Jerry picked up the phone it was dead again and he was ready to kick some tail. It was after midnight, but he was going to get it straight with the guy right then. "Let me go down," I said. "He's not mad at me and he's already had a run-in with you." Jerry didn't like the idea, but he let me handle it—something we would both regret by morning.

"Our phone is dead again," I told the clerk when I arrived at the desk, "and we're gonna need a wakeup call in the morning. Let's try to watch it, huh?"

"All right, all right," he said. "I'll turn it on. Is that other ——— still up there?"

I stared into his dark eyes and reached across the counter to touch his forearm for emphasis. "That ——— up there, as you call him, happens to be my brother, and if you're gonna use that kind of language about him, we're gonna have us some trouble."

He was massive, husky, and probably six-foot-four. When he wrenched his arm away and took a swing at me, I leaned back and he couldn't reach me over the counter. "What's the matter with you?" I shouted.

"Nothin's wrong with me," he said, "but you just wait right there and somethin's gonna be wrong with you." He rummaged in a drawer and I instinctively reached for a table ashtray, one of those huge, heavy jobs made of glass.

The black man raced to the end of the counter, kicked open the swinging door, and charged me with a straight razor. He was upon me quickly, slashing my neck and fingers as I tried to shield myself. It happened so fast I forgot I had a weapon. He jabbed and slashed, pushing me back toward the front door and ramming the blade into my left side, digging through the rib cage and into my lung. As I gasped for air a voice inside told me, "Act now or it's over."

I took a wide wild swipe with the ashtray, crashing it into the side of his head and breaking the glass at a murderous angle. He stumbled back, shook his head, and charged again. I bashed him in the face with what was left of the ashtray, tearing a huge chunk of flesh from his cheekbone from his eye to his chin. Two bellmen grabbed him from behind and a man who had been dozing in the lobby grabbed me.

As his friends struggled to drag him into a back room,

the clerk screamed, "I'm gonna kill you, you white ———!"

"You're gonna kill *me?*" I yelled with a sarcastic laugh. "It looks to me like *you're* the one who's hurt! Come back out here and I'll finish you off!"

I was crazy with rage, but the man who held me said, "Hey, enough people have been hurt."

"He's the only one hurt," I said.

"You've been stabbed," he said. "Look."

Blood was squirting from me like water from a sprinkler. I felt no pain yet, but suddenly I was weak and dizzy. I staggered toward the elevator. "I've got to get to my brother."

"You don't have time to get to your brother, man," he said. "You've got to get to the hospital."

I don't remember how he got me there; in fact, I never even found out who he was. But I arrived at the emergency room at about 2:30 A.M. and was wheeled right into the room where the black guy was being sewn up. They wheeled me right back out and into another room, where I was left unattended until morning. When I could manage enough breath to move at all—I was too weak to call out for anyone—I gave myself oxygen from a tank against the wall. All night my brain whirled as I fought to stay alive and to piece together what had happened.

It was several days before even my doctor thought I would pull through. My family and my fiancée, Gloria, offered to come and be with me, but I assured them I would be all right, not really knowing for sure myself. I just lay there as quietly as I could for weeks, trying not to exert any motion that would cause me to breathe harder than I was able.

Even when it became obvious that I would live, no one could say whether or not I'd sing again. My thoughts leading up to the Griffin show seemed ironic now. I thought the national exposure, combined with my current hit, "Eyes of a New York Woman," would catapult me to another great year like I'd had in 1966.

I had been named the most promising male vocalist and enjoyed a half dozen hits while traveling with Dick Clark. But when I quit recording good stuff and quit spending as much time in the studio as I should have, sales dropped and I had a miserable failure of a year in 1967. Jerry and I had moved from our home in Texas to Memphis to record, and "New York Woman" had proved that it was the right move. Things were on the upswing again. But now this.

It hurt Jerry to see me in such bad shape. We had been through a lot together. He's just a year and a half older than I am and had stuck up for me all my life. I knew he was wishing he had handled the desk clerk from the beginning and I was sure he still wanted revenge.

Growing up with Jerry in and around Houston in the early 1940s and '50s was something I wouldn't trade for anything. He had contracted polio when he was five and the treatment in those days was hot towels applied to every inch of the body. Somehow during his treatment, Jerry suffered damage to his inner ear which cost him some of his capacity to hear certain sounds. For instance, when someone says the word *school,* Jerry hears *stool.* He now pronounces words the way he hears them, so what people think is a speech impediment is actually a hearing problem.

You get used to it after a few sentences and he's not hard to understand. Most people find that his speech has an endearing childlike quality about it. I like to think of it as God's trademark on him.

He's a great guy who'll do anything for you, and because of his partial hearing loss, he reads a person more by the look on his face than by the tone of voice. The people in the circles I travel in think he's the greatest. Everybody who's ever met him on the road or in the studio knows he's a compassionate, fair person with a legend of his own all over the country (even if he can be a little crotchety sometimes!)

His hearing problem may have been one of the reasons Jerry grew up as such a tough guy. He wasn't picked on too much over it because he always knew how to handle himself. He fought a lot even into adulthood, but that has mellowed out with the years and he no longer looks for trouble.

We fought each other often as kids, but as we grew older we made a pact that we would always stay friends, no matter if we agreed on everything or not. We saw that our dad was not as close to his brothers as he might have been, and we didn't want anything to come between us.

We thought Dad was all the movie stars rolled into one. He never made much money in the air-conditioning business, and we moved around quite a bit, but, in my eyes, my dad was right up there with Robert Taylor and Humphrey Bogart. He had a drinking problem that got worse with the years, and he died in his early fifties, but even his philosophy of life intrigued me. He always said he wanted to live hard and die young and leave a beautiful memory.

I adopted the same idea, thinking it was romantic. It may even have been one of the reasons that drugs seemed so attractive to me at first. There was something about the fun and the risk . . . which may have been why Dad first started to drink. That wasn't the only thing I inherited from Dad.

He would have been surprised at the number of people who showed up at his funeral in 1971, because no matter how much people tried to tell him they loved him, he couldn't believe it. He was fun-loving, yet introverted, and certainly had an inferiority complex. In later years, those very same characteristics would surface in me. When I needed love the most, I had it from people who really cared. But I just could not believe it.

Being the second of three children—I have a younger sister—I enjoyed neither the favored position of the oldest, nor the attention of being the baby, so my shyness came through early. I was so naïve that I didn't even cuss until I was in junior high! It wasn't that the family was so straight or anything. I just wasn't that worldly wise. When I had to say a bad word for the first time to join a club, I thought I was real hot stuff.

There was something about us Thomases that was unlike a lot of poor people. In spite of our lack of money and not having much of anything else, we had good attitudes about life in general. Oh, we had our quarrels and our scenes, but we didn't resign ourselves to being trash, like too many poor people do. We knew that somehow we'd pull through, so we kept hoping and waiting and expecting our break to come. We were gonna make something of ourselves. Everything was gonna be all right.

We moved to a house on Allen-Genoa Road when I was about twelve. I learned how a little baseball equipment could make me some friends; and it also marked my first encounter with God.

2   the "Triumphs"

There was a Baptist church across the street from us on Allen-Genoa Road, and when Jerry and I waltzed over there with our baseball equipment one Saturday, the kids playing ball thought we were really great.

It wasn't long before I felt obligated to accept the invitations of my new friends to go to their church. The sermon about Jesus loving me and dying on the cross for my sins was new to me. When the pastor said that Jesus rose from the dead and wanted people to receive him into their hearts and lives, I was on the spot.

Here I was, a guest. All these kids seemed to be Christians, and I felt they wanted me to go forward down the aisle to receive Christ. So I did. How sincere I was, I can't really say. How sincere you have to be when you ask Jesus to save you I don't know either. For all I know, God may have started his work in my life right then.

There was no talk of commitment or living for him or anything, and my life didn't change. So, I always assumed that it didn't take. I do remember running home and telling my mother, "Hey, I got saved today. I've been born again." She said nothing. She just looked embarrassed.

I don't know when she became a Christian, but I know now that she loves the Lord. She was a fantastic example of clean living, if not Christianity, when I was growing up. She was very much like her own father, a very straight guy. I was shocked once just to hear him say he was going to go to the barn to draw some water instead of saying he was going to the bathroom—that's how straight he was. He was so far from even cussing that I thought such a comment was risqué, coming from him.

Mother was an example too in the way she treated Dad. His drinking caused him occasionally to be violent and unreasonable, yet she never left him. She loved him through it all and treated him with dignity. I think that's why he was able to go on supporting his family and being a father to us in spite of his drinking. Even when he hurt Mother or us kids, she wouldn't let us talk bad about him.

It was around this time that I remember sitting in the back seat of my Uncle Jack's car listening to the radio. Uncle Jack was telling us about a new singer named Elvis Presley. I could hardly comprehend what radio music was all about, but when I heard Hank Williams sing "Settin' the Woods on Fire," I just had to have my Aunt Bonnie copy down the words for me. She had some of his other records, and I learned them and sang them around the house constantly.

From then on, music was always in the back of my mind. It surfaced again when we moved to 34th Street, not far from the Temple Oaks Baptist Church. We were invited to go by some neighborhood kids, and I was immediately impressed by the pastor. His name was Jack Blackwell, and I thought he was just great. He preached about God and salvation and Jesus, but to him, being a Christian meant more than just avoiding hellfire and brimstone. It was there that I first started singing publicly, not as a soloist but in quartets and the choir. Certain families in that church really cared for Jerry and me, and we made friends with a good Christian kid named Ernest Clinton.

He was a long, tall, fun-loving guy who ran with us. We did everything together. Long after we had moved away from there I had fond memories of good times with ol' Ernest.

It seemed Jerry and I were at the church every day for one thing or another. If we weren't playing Ping Pong in the basement we were mowing the pastor's lawn. I started learning a few things about the Bible through sheer exposure. One Sunday I started feeling convicted about my relationship with Jesus. I still didn't understand it all, but I knew somehow that I had to get right with God.

I had no concept of sin—unless sin was kissing girls in the back seat of a car—nor what it could do to my life. I just felt guilty, and that's why I went forward again. This time I really wanted to mean it, but again I learned so little about how to live a Christian life that it made no immediate real impact on me.

It's likely that more happened between God and me then than I knew. When I think of the odds against my surviving the thousands upon thousands of drugs I poured into my body, I know that God spared me for a reason. All during my later drug years, God kept coming up. It wasn't that I just wanted to kick drugs and clean up my life; it was God. I knew I was being drawn back to him. I believe he laid a claim on me as a child and wouldn't let me go.

We moved a little farther away from Temple Oaks Baptist when I was in high school and I went to church less frequently, finally dropping out when I felt I'd outgrown it.

Jerry and I began playing more and more league baseball and I picked up the nickname B. J. instead of Billy Joe because there were so many Billys in our league.

When Jerry and I finally landed at Lamar Consolidated High School in Rosenberg, Texas, we played on the baseball team that lost every game but one, and that one was a no-hit shutout pitched by Jerry.

It was good that I had taken an interest in music by that time, because while the baseball team was racking up a record of one win against fourteen losses, we weren't being taught that losing wasn't all that bad. I could have used a good lesson in how to lose. The summer league teams we had played on had all been winners. When we began to lose, I really got down on myself.

The coach had his head down as low as we did, so there was nothing gained from the experience. I took it personally. It didn't make me less of a person to lose, but I didn't know that. I started thinking that I must not be very good if our team couldn't win a game. It soured me on baseball and also left me high and dry later in life when I lost on stage, in my marriage, and in my business.

I had never learned how to keep losses in perspective or how to turn them into advantages. I was patterned to assume that if I didn't do well on stage, then I wasn't a good human being. Since I've become a Christian, I've learned not to take the music so seriously. Strangely, though I'm now even more competitive, more quality-oriented and success-minded, I have finally realized that you can't put too much stock in a self-glorifying art.

I want to make the best music I've ever made. I want it to be right and sound good whether it sells or not. I've been blessed with a voice and I want to use it well, but I'll not take every performance so seriously that I judge my character by it. That would be as bad as thinking that after a great performance, I am a better person.

Music or fame or money will not fill the void that only God can. I know.

Well, I soon realized that I would never be a great baseball player. If I was, I would have helped Lamar win some games. I went out for the team again the next year, but my heart wasn't in it and I got kicked off for breaking curfew. Somehow I thought I'd get even by taking up smoking, and that put me into a whole different group than the athletes. But then Jerry and I had never really felt part of that school anyway. When we had moved into the area from Houston, it was months before anyone would give us the time of day.

I sang in the choir and had become a fan of Jackie Wilson, a rhythm and blues singer with a fantastic range. I listened to him on the radio and on records every chance I got, wondering how anyone could sing that good. And he even made a living at it!

We all loved Elvis and Hank Williams, but I think Wilson had the biggest influence on me. I couldn't believe what he could do with his voice. I've always tried to do more with a note than just hit it, because I remembered how he could sing so high and so right, really putting something into it.

The ice finally broke for Jerry and me at school the day a Mexican kid hit me on the head from behind with a choir book. Jerry was so mad he just jumped up and cold-cocked the guy. Knocked him smooth out. Suddenly we were befriended not only by white kids who hated Mexicans, but by Mexicans who knew the troublemaker was at fault anyway. Jerry got a reputation that wouldn't quit. He became known around Lamar as a guy who would be a true friend, but also as a guy to not mess with if he wasn't your friend.

He refused to go to special classes or sit in the front of the room so he could hear better, because he just wanted to be one of the guys. When he got the idea that few people around there thought he would ever graduate, it just made him stick with it and get that diploma. Jerry knew that just because polio had affected his hearing and thus his speech, that didn't make him any less a man.

He still sticks up for me verbally. Even before I became well known, people thought I was stuck up or arrogant, which I'm sure I was. Inside I was shy, but since I was a singer who didn't have much to say except to be funny, I came off the wrong way. People would tell Jerry, "Man, I don't like your brother. He's a smart aleck."

But Jerry really knew me and understood my personality, so he set them straight and made me a lot of friends that might otherwise never have had anything to do with me.

I was not a popular guy; in fact, there was only a small circle of Jerry's and my friends that I would open up to. The choir director thought I was just a goof-off, and though I was president of the choir for two years, I failed choir as a course! I was paranoid and introverted and pretty much kept to myself.

That's why I panicked when Jerry told me he had arranged an audition for me as lead singer in a new local band, the Triumphs. He knew I enjoyed singing with the radio and with records and all that, so he told the drummer that the Triumphs should hear me sing. In fact, more than twenty years later I found out that he told them I sang like Ricky Nelson.

I still don't know how he talked me into it, but he dragged me over there and I gave it a shot. I had no control. Besides being nervous, I had never mastered all that I had been told in choir about taking a deep breath and supporting yourself with lung power. I knew all right what I should be doing, but I couldn't pull it off yet. I just strained and sang loud and did the best I could. The band wasn't much better, and they liked my singing, so I accepted their invitation to join them.

Roy Head, an already accomplished singer, sat in on my audition and told me he liked my singing. That gave me a little confidence, but still at performances I just stood motionless behind the microphone and sang my lungs out. I was scared to death.

We'd rehearse for a few hours and I wouldn't be able to talk for two days. Luckily I had a strong throat and survived all that strain through the years until I learned how to sing without exerting so much pressure on my vocal cords. That has saved me a lot of grief and the only thing that gets to me now is fatigue after too many shows in too few nights, or singing in a dry air environment like the desert.

I was a junior at Lamar High in January of 1958 when we Triumphs played our first gigs. We played a few small dances at the teen canteen and places like that, but when we put on a dance at the American Legion Hall, it seemed everybody in town came to see us.

We had a tremendous crowd and they loved it, but we were terrible. All we knew were twelve songs and by the end of the evening, everyone else there knew them too. We must've done "Johnny B. Goode" a half dozen times.

I wore red slacks and a pink coat, an absolutely outrageous outfit. But it was great fun and we each made three dollars for the night. We gave the money to the mother of one of the guys and she made us some shirts with *The Triumphs* embroidered on the backs. We had arrived.

For some reason, people soon started to shun me. Maybe it was jealousy. Maybe it was my shyness coming through as arrogance again; I don't know. They treated me as if I were some big-headed dude, and surely I was to some extent. I had never been anybody before, so maybe I thought I was due a season in the sun. I was a bit overbearing.

When I get into something, it becomes an obsession with me. Soon I found myself out of high school, still singing and performing and not wanting to stop. I wasn't thinking about a career or anything, but right then it was the only thing I wanted to do. That attitude was characteristic of my whole life. When I get on something—even drugs—I go all the way. The other guys had graduated too, of course, and one by one they were dropping out to go off to college or to pursue some sensible career. I was still living at home, working other jobs during the week, and pulling in a few hundred dollars a year singing with the Triumphs on weekends. I tried junior college for one semester but instead of studying, all I did was drink and raise Cain. I couldn't see music as a secondary thing like the other guys could.

Every year we made at least one trip to Garner State Park, ninety miles from San Antonio and not far from the Mexican border. It became an annual habit to make a run into Mexico to score some cheap grass or pills (it was always available and cheap south of the border) and get blasted. We'd do the drugs and stay up all night staring at each other and laughing. We thought it was great fun.

For most of the guys it was just a kick, like smoking behind the barn or coming home drunk from a party. It was stupid and they shouldn't have done it, but they grew out of it and it became just one of those silly memories we all have. But for me it was never just a silly memory. I was never one who could do just a few pills and laugh it off the next day. If I had a dozen uppers, I did a dozen uppers. If I had more, I did more.

It was a peek into my future, and I never even saw it. I rarely abused drugs (except for those trips to Garner State Park) while living at home, but my day would come.

3　　　78 with a bullet

The Triumphs had been together for about three years when we cut our first single, "The Lazy Man." It was big only in the Houston area until we played at Garner State Park again and somebody got the record onto the park juke box. When the kids went back to their hometowns, they started asking for it in stores.

Before long we had all the engagements we could handle, and after a couple of more local hits, we released a song written by Mark Charron called "I Got a Feelin'." We cut it in the studio of a guy named Charlie Booth who thought it had more of a national feel to it. To help sales, he said, he put my name on the label: "B. J. Thomas and the Triumphs." He did it with my permission, of course, but not theirs.

The band and I never really got along too well, and this didn't help. Down deep we loved each other, but we argued all the time; in fact, I think I had a fistfight with every one of the guys at one time or another. It might have been over girls or after getting on each other's case too much at rehearsal. We didn't need much of a reason.

It seemed like every guy in the band thought he should be the leader—one because he originated the band, another because he thought of the name. I thought I should be because I was the singer. We all had our reasons but no one ever really led.

We were our own booking agents and played a lot of big engagements, including some shows sponsored by KILT in Houston. Playing with big name stars like Roy Orbison convinced me that I was really gonna dig the music business, especially if we could get even bigger and more well known.

We weren't making much money off our records because the guys recording us were sharks. We were just fish to them and too naïve to know what was happening.

Naïveté was my life back then. Jerry and I were running with some bad dudes from Houston and we were always goofing off and getting into some kind of trouble. We were drinking and fighting and getting tossed in jail. Once we even broke into an interstate transport truck just for fun. At least I thought it was fun.

We never got into serious trouble or got big police records or anything, but after a while I began to feel more hollow with each hangover the morning after. After we had really had a blowout one night in 1963, Jerry and I spent the night at the home of a friend, Foster Savley.

I woke up bleary-eyed and with a headache. Foster came in as I was sitting on the edge of the bed, running my fingers through my hair and trying to get the room to come into focus.

"Hey, I bet I can tell you somethin' you don't know," he said.

I wasn't in the mood for games, and anyway, I didn't even know my own name that early in the morning. "What's that?" I mumbled.

"Ernest is dead."

"What? Ernest Clinton?"

"Yeah. Killed in a wreck last night."

I sat there for a few seconds before it sank in. My old friend Ernest. Foster left me alone to cry. Here I was, twenty-one years old, still living at home, singing in a band, and goofing off every night. For Ernest it was all over. *What have you done with your life?* I asked myself.

The whole day was a bummer. Everything was gray and all I could think about was Ernest. I hadn't seen him for a long time but I could clearly remember how he could play such a good game of basketball. And how he could jump up and kick an eight-foot ceiling, he was that tall.

But mostly, I just thought how young he was to be gone and that I could go anytime too with all the nonsense I was into. I had done nothing with my life. I knew I had to get right with God, and to me that meant no more cussing, drinking, smoking, doing dope, or even playing in the band. I called one of the guys to tell him and he didn't even flinch. "Do you know Dean Scott's number?" was his reaction. Here I was quitting the Triumphs after five years and he just wanted the phone number of another singer.

When I saw a couple of other members of the Triumphs I tried to tell them that I was reevaluating my life and felt I needed to make a commitment to God. They had a good laugh and I was hurt, but I just left it at that.

I started going to Temple Oaks Baptist again, and this time I really got involved. When I tried to stand up and tell what had happened to me, I became so emotional that I cried and embarrassed myself. I wished I hadn't tried.

For six months I worked in a clothing store and did every thing I knew how to do to be happy and fulfilled. But it didn't work. I was straight, but I was going nuts without my music and my old friends and my kind of fun. I know now that just trying to clean up your life does not bring you closer to God or make you happy, but back then I had no idea what was wrong.

One night I threw my new life away and did all the things I hadn't done for months with some friends. My commitment was over, no good, a failure. I joined a band called the Jades who were recording for Charlie Booth. They had been struggling, but they became popular real quick, which was a much-needed boost to my ego.

I had been with the Jades for about six months when I got a call from Teddy Minsek, the drummer for the Triumphs. He and his father were booking the band and they wanted me to come and talk with them at their house. Before I was even seated, I said, "If you are going to ask me to come back to the Triumphs, the answer is yes." I really missed those guys. It had been almost a year.

"That's what we want," they said. It was a good day that led to a couple of more good years with the Triumphs. We still got on each other's nerves and all, but being back with them was like being home again.

Songwriter Mark Charron moved into my parents' house with me and wrote a lot of our material. He was a great guitarist and would play while I sang for my father. I had just fallen in love again with Hank Williams' song "I'm So Lonesome," after seeing Williams' life story in the movie *Your Cheatin' Heart*. I could really get into singing it, and when we did it for Dad it made him cry.

I worked it into our shows and added an affected ending to it that I've become known for. It's my own little vocal trick that adds a nice touch people seem to enjoy. I used it in the recording studio a few months later.

We were cutting Mark's "Hey Judy" for Huey Meaux (better known as the Crazy Cajun) on the Pacemaker label, and we needed a tune for the B side of the record. I

suggested "I'm So Lonesome," and producer Charlie Booth
cued the machines. We ran it down a few times, but the
trumpet player kept messing up his part. By then I was
losing interest in spending so much time on a song for the B
side. "Aw, forget it," I said. "Let's try something else."

With that, Charlie came out of the control booth. "Hey,
B.," he said, "let's not forget it. You should hear it."

We tried it a few more times, finally telling the trumpeter
that he had one more chance to do it right. None of us were
terribly experienced in the studio, but we knew we'd have
to go to something else unless we could do this one just
right. It was a little shaky, but it was right. When the record was pressed we couldn't wait to take "Hey Judy" up to
Bob White, the program director at KILT.

We were disappointed to find that he didn't like it. "I
can't play that one," he said. "I don't think it's got it. But
while you're here, let me hear the other side." We played
"I'm So Lonesome" for him and his eyes lit up. "Man, I
can play that one!" he said.

We had no idea what a national hit record was supposed
to sound like, but we said, "Well, ok, great," and left it
with him. Within three weeks it was the number one song
in Houston.

Steve Tyrell, a young promoter friend at Scepter Records,
heard the song and talked Scepter into picking it up and
releasing it nationally. I didn't know what that could mean,
but we were glad to let them try it.

Two weeks later I was awakened by an old friend who
kicked open my bedroom door and waved around a copy

of *Cashbox* magazine. "Look, man," he shouted. "You've got a smash!"

Sure enough, there was "I'm So Lonesome," listed 78th in the country out of the top 100 pop songs of the week. It had a bullet next to it, signifying that it was an extremely fast seller. I had hardly been aware of *Cashbox* magazine, because nothing we had ever done had appeared in it before, but I found out soon enough what it all meant.

Within a few days I had invitations to play an engagement up north and another to work for three days with soul singer James Brown. The Triumphs, who had not been invited, were not at all happy about the turn of events. When I got an offer to travel with Dick Clark's troupe of several acts, I told the band I could get them between twelve and fifteen hundred dollars a week, but they refused. It wasn't that the money wasn't good, it was just that they didn't like the fact that all of a sudden they were just a band and I was the big shot.

Of course, promoters don't care if a band signs or not. They sign the lead singer and find musicians as they travel. I really loved the Triumphs and I think they cared for me too, but that was the end of us. I couldn't pass up the offer. If they had stayed with me I would still be earning them decent livings, but I know that sounds arrogant, and I can't really blame them for not taking the risk.

Here I was, just starting to get national exposure from the remake of an old Hank Williams tune that we almost didn't record and which wound up on the B side of a record nobody ever heard. Now I was traipsing off with Dick

Clark. Who knew I'd ever make it? Lots of singers on that
tour are nowhere now, so maybe the Triumphs were better
off choosing to let me be the big city guy. They stayed
closer to home and never had to endure the drug years
with me, so it would be hard to convince them that they
should have done otherwise.

With the help of an arranger, Glen Spreen, I got together
another band from the Houston area. In 1966 I would
travel with Gene Pitney, Linn Berry, Paul Revere and the
Raiders, and many other acts that toured with Dick Clark.
We had hits with "Mama," "Bring Back the Time," and
"Tomorrow Never Comes," and "Billy and Sue" was a
million seller.

I was making money I had never even dreamed of. By
1967 I had sold four and a half million records and was
making $2,500 a night for singing four songs. With no
management or counsel—at least that I'd listen to—I was
taking the money in cash, carrying it around in my pockets,
and spending it as fast as it came in. Believe me, it rolled in
fast.

Hundreds of thousands of dollars from record royalties
and tens of thousands from personal appearances went for
cars and clothes and gifts and extravagant things I didn't
need or want. I was drunk with the freedom to have anything and everything I saw. I had no checking or savings
accounts and would not have known how to go about
making an investment if one had stared me in the face.
With all that money pouring in, I was broke by the time
the next check came.

It was while on the road that I first started taking drugs for other than an occasional kick. If I had a sore throat from singing eighty-seven days out of ninety, someone would slip me a pill and I'd feel great. It seemed to me I was singing better than ever, and I had completely forgotten my sore throat. I thought the pills were great and started taking them before every show to give me an edge.

There was so much to learn from the oldtimers and the newcomers alike. I picked up a lot of things from the long, hard tour. Like the fact that you don't shave right before a show because you might cut yourself. And you don't have to shine your shoes if the stage has footlights because no one will see your feet anyway.

I also learned the intriguing competitive games that musicians and singers play. We are a fraternity and we all love and respect each other, but down deep each wants to be the best in the show, and nothing gives us more satisfaction than drawing the longest, loudest applause of the night.

But being on the road ground me down. The hardest part was being away from the family for the first extended period in my life. I should have taken Jerry with me. He had been with the Triumphs most of the time—in an unofficial capacity—and I really missed him. I had left for the road the happiest guy in the world, but a year later you wouldn't have recognized me. I was miserable. I had been away from the recording studios too long, and that's where good selling records are made. For four or five days' work I had sold millions of records. And though the immediate applause on the road is gratifying, it doesn't pay the bills like a hit record does. My sales plummeted and it took me a while to figure out why.

I thought everything I recorded would be a hit after the first smashes, but it doesn't work that way. You need to stay close to the writers and the producers and be in the studio when the hit songs become available. The success and the money had been like a miracle to me and my family. It overwhelmed us, but when the records quit selling, I thought it was over.

Too young to be a has-been, and not liking the taste of it, I returned to Houston, got an apartment, and sat around feeling sorry for myself. The best I could pull in was an occasional $300 performance. When I was tired I found myself doing more and more drugs.

But soon I would meet Gloria and I would have to keep the pills part of my life hidden from her. And they would almost do me in.

4   Gloria

Houston's Southwest Freeway was almost deserted Sunday night, September 17, 1967. Gloria Richardson, a recent high school graduate and a department store model, had agreed to take a ride with a friend who was feeling down. John (not his real name) just wanted someone to talk to.

Gloria had to work the next day and considered not going. She finally agreed to a short ride.

John had just pulled onto the expressway and had accelerated to about 70 m.p.h. in the far right lane when

Gloria saw a car parked ahead of them. She was certain John had seen it when he slowly angled left into the middle lane. He had not realized, however, that the car was stopped, and at the last instant pulled back into the right lane behind it again.

Gloria screamed, but John never had time to hit the brake. They slammed into the back of the parked car, spun around crazily and rammed the front, bouncing off and crashing into the car yet again. With each collision Gloria was thrust through the front windshield and then wrenched over the back of the seat and through the window again.

When the car finally stopped, teetering on the guardrail over a twenty-foot drop to another highway, Gloria lay on the floorboard facing the engine. Her lips, nearly severed by her teeth, were stuck inside her mouth. Two teeth were gone, her jawbone was broken, her knee had been mutilated by a tape machine under the dash. Her face was unrecognizable, a mass of deep lacerations, the forehead laid back across the top of her head.

Her body was numb to the pain but her mind raced. Hold on, hold on, hold on, hold on, *she told herself.* Oh, it hurts to hold on. It's hard, but if you let go, you're going to die. *Then, in her mind, she let go. But she did not die.*

John, who had suffered a sprained ankle, limped to her door which hung open. "Oh, my God!" he cried as he tried to pull her out. She stood for a while and collapsed. John walked around in a daze. It seemed like forever before someone stopped. The night was rainy, the ground bone cold. Gloria felt cool liquid all over her face.

Three nurses on their way to work saw the wreckage and

carted John and Gloria to the hospital. On the way, Gloria
lay with her head in the lap of one of the women, her
head wrapped in an already blood-drenched shirt. "I'm
hurt," she said, clawing at her own face.

"No, you're not," the nurse said. "You're fine."

"I'm bleeding!"

"No, you're not. You're fine."

When she awoke in Memorial Hospital facing weeks of
recuperation and surgery (400 stitches were required to
reconstruct her face), her reaction was: "Nothing can stay
wrong for long. I'll deal with it."

And she would. She would deal with it the way she had
dealt with rejection as a child—the only unsupervised girl
in the neighborhood. She would deal with it the way she
had dealt with moving so much that she attended twenty-
two different schools before graduating three months before
the accident. She would deal with it the way she dealt
with people who thought she should stay in her class—
whatever that was—on the other side of the tracks, in a
trailer park, just surviving.

She had already moved away from home and was on her
own. No one would make her decisions for her. No one
would be there when she was in trouble. She had people
who cared, but no one who could help her any more than
she could help herself. And so she would deal with it.

She was in mummy bandages and couldn't walk for
three weeks. The first steps she took were out the front
door, back to work—not as a model any more—but as
a clerk.

People thought she was brave, but she was scared and

*lonely. Practicality was the name of her game. She simply
knew that her future was in her own hands. She could give
up, or she could get back into the action.*

*And that was the girl B. J. Thomas met at Van's Ballroom
in Houston a few weeks later.*

When I first saw her in that dimly lit place, I thought it
was my sister, Judy. "It's getting late," I said. "You'd better
get home."

"I may look like your sister," she told me. "But I'm not."

I asked her to go to a party with me and she was real
straight with me, not mean. She said, "Look, if you just
want a showhorse to flaunt, I want to tell you right now
that I've just been in a wreck. I've got scars on my face
that turn colors in this weather, and I'm missing two teeth.
When you see me in the light, if you don't want to take me
home, you don't have to."

I couldn't wait to prove to her that it wouldn't make any
difference to me. I was already in love with her straight-
forwardness. We saw each other that night and virtually
every night until New Year's Eve.

Gloria was different. Besides having a mind of her own,
she was not loose like other girls I had known. We would
have our hassles and spats, but it was obvious to me that
we were in love. The only hitch was that I was still doing
pills, and she didn't know. Something had to break soon
in my career too. I was tired of being broke.

Jerry and I finally decided to pack up and move to
Memphis where I could start recording again and try to

get something back on the charts. It was hard to leave Gloria.

She thought it would be the end of us, that I would dump her and find someone else in Memphis. "You'll never be able to forget me," she said in her typical fashion—which I loved. "Anybody you have a relationship with from now on will be a compromise." She knew when something was real and when it wasn't, and she knew my love for her was, even though I had never even told her I loved her.

I had no intention of throwing her over. I came back to see her as often as I could and called her often. During one visit in February, we became engaged to be married. Being apart was hard for us, but when I finally recorded another hit, it looked like the best thing for my career—at least temporarily.

We didn't cut any hit records in our first recording session in Memphis, but we did meet producer Chips Moman of the American Studios recording group. He had been in some good combos and was a terrific guitar player. But what a producer! I knew that if we could stay close to him and somehow hook up with him again when we had hit material, things would click. My career didn't have to be over.

Jerry and I hung around and hung around until finally I cut "The Eyes of a New York Woman" in early 1968. Boy, it was great to have a hit again and a reason to take to the road. We traveled around in a '66 Corvette, and we had money again. Promoters made sure a band was waiting for us at each one-night stand, so things were pretty simple.

I'll never forget the day we played the Mid-South State Fair in Meridian, Mississippi, and I had to follow a singin' pig. Literally. A white pig that traveled with a big fat guy in overalls would grunt the tune of "Sittin' on the Dock of the Bay." It was one of the funniest acts I've ever seen.

One guy in the audience that day booed me after every song. I'm sure he liked the pig better, and I finally realized why when I got a look at the heckler. He was a promoter who had booked me a few months before, and I had stood him up. I had showed up to rehearse with his band, but they were so bad I could only work up about three songs with them. "I'm goin' back to the hotel to shower and shave," I told them, and then I just hopped in my car and headed back to Memphis. Those were the days.

My engagement to Gloria and the invitation to appear on the Merv Griffin Show in New York seemed like just more icing on the cake of '68. Gloria remembers:

I knew B. J. was in New York that night and somehow I had a strange feeling about it. I was out with girlfriends but I came home early, just knowing something was going to happen. It was hard to sleep, but I finally dropped off. Jerry called at about five o'clock in the morning.

He said B. J. had been hurt bad. "How is he?" I asked. "He might die."

I was just bummed out for days, but B. J. didn't want me to come to New York. I felt totally helpless, not knowing if he would live and unable to do anything about it. I

*wasn't myself again until I saw him. He wasn't himself
again for months.*

For a long time I could hardly talk, and for sure I couldn't
sing. When I tried rehearsing again after several months I
thought I was going to die. I went to a doctor in Memphis
who is known among famous singers for always having
pills available. He provided all the uppers I wanted.

I had forgotten how great pills were. They gave me energy, helped me perform, made me feel good. I was enjoying myself again. Now that I had a pipeline to all the
drugs I could afford, I couldn't stop taking them.

Jerry always tried to stay off pills while we were working
because he had to take care of me on the road. It got to
where I was taking pills before and after shows; then I
thought it would be even better to take pills half a day
before a show. If they wore off too soon, I would take twice
as many to duplicate the high.

I kept Jerry busy. He had to stay with me, keep me
straight, help me make appointments. I would be straight
for awhile, then get right back to the pills. If the pills got
me into a talking mood I could talk for days at a time on
anything and everything anybody would care to hear about
and a lot of stuff they didn't. It was murder on my voice,
it being low to begin with.

Sometimes a bunch of people would get together and get
high and just sit around and talk. Sometimes it was serious
and sometimes it wasn't. When it was serious, they were
real depressing, downer sessions, I'll tell you. Our bodies

were under such strain that honesty would come out and we would talk about all of our problems. What a bummer.

In the past I had played around with pills, taking a few too many now and then for a quick high. I had gotten blasted at a few parties, sure, but I was still in the minor leagues then. I'm not saying that doing any pills is OK—just that before this time I had not really been into pill addiction. And beware those who tell you there is no such thing. Either they have never done the number of pills I started doing, or they are addicted and don't know it.

Some people were able to do some pills and then stay away from them for a few days. Not me. I had to do all the pills around whenever they were available. Jerry pleaded with the Memphis doctor to quit giving me pills.

A few months before we were married I began telling Gloria that I was no good for her, that she was more than I deserved. I never told her about the drugs, and she never suspected. But it wasn't long after we were married that she discovered the bad side of me she had never seen.

Ours was a tragic love story. We were so hopelessly, illogically in love that we couldn't see straight. Our love had no foundation, no sense, just romance. In years to come we would come to a dozen places and crises that should have broken us up for good, but our love would suck us back together. Only twice would we even separate, but through it all, we would love each other.

Four months after we were married Gloria became pregnant. Five months later we moved to New York for an extended booking at the Copacabana on the wings of my

Big brother Jerry and
B(illy) J(oe) Thomas.

Thomas family snapshot:
Mom and Dad, Judy, B. J., Jerry.

Sixth-grader
B. J. Thomas.

Getting ready
for high school
graduation, but
thinking only
of music.

The Triumphs. Left to right: Fred Carney, Donald Drachenberg, Gary Koepen, Denver Zatyka, Teddy Mensik, B. J. Thomas, Tom Griffith, and Tim Griffith. It was B. J.'s single "I'm So Lonesome," recorded with the Triumphs, that first got him onto the national charts.

1966 Male Vocalist of the Year, on tour with Dick Clark.

B. J. Thomas publicity photo (Don Perry Productions)

Recording session.
Above: A & R Vice
President for WORD
Music and Records
Buddy Huey, B. J., and
Chris Christian, pro-
ducer of *Home Where I
Belong,* B. J.'s first al-
bum for WORD. Right:
Standing behind B. J.
are (l to r) his manager,
Don Perry, B. J.'s
brother Jerry, and
Buddy Huey.

1971: Between horror
scenes, happy times.
B. J. and Paige.

1977: Paige and
her daddy, home
to stay.

Steve Aune of *Gospel Trade* magazine in interview at Dallas-Fort Worth Airport with B. J., Gloria, and Paige.

Seemingly separated from Gloria for good, B. J. called long distance anyway. "She was more at peace than I had ever heard her." At Dallas press conference, Gloria shares what she'd found.

"This old earth is really pretty to a mind
that's been cleared by the power of God. . . ."
(Phil Van Duivendyk photo)

current hit, "Hooked on a Feelin'." The money was rolling in again.

Steve Tyrell became my manager and Foster Savley was my road man for a while when Jerry took some time off. With Jerry gone, I got so heavily into pills that nothing he could do when he returned would do any good. I was past straightening out, and by late 1969 I knew I was hooked.

I was an addict. I wouldn't admit it to Gloria, but then neither she nor anyone else wanted to face that fact. I don't know if it would have done any good or not, but not one person in all this time looked me in the eye and said, "B. J., you are a drug addict." I loved the drugs more than anything else, and no matter how many hours and days of grief it caused my young wife, I could not, I would not quit.

The biggest boost ever in my career came when I was asked to sing "Raindrops Keep Fallin' On My Head," Burt Bacharach's song for the movie *Butch Cassidy and the Sundance Kid*. It was to become a gold single, a gold album, a Grammy and Oscar nominee, and the number one hit of the year. I was back in gear, commanding top dollar everywhere I went, selling records like crazy and rolling in literally millions of dollars.

During the next six years I would gross over $13 million, but I never once got my head up out of the mud. I was bogged down in drugs and everything was a failure. In spite of records that sold three million copies, I was troubled and insane because I couldn't go home and be happy. I was as famous as any singer could ever hope to be, but there was nowhere to rest my head.

Something was missing and I didn't know what it was.

5   horror scenes

Our daughter Paige was born early in 1970, and I was named number one male vocalist of the year, yet it was the first of the half dozen worst years of my life and I was more dead than alive. I could hardly have cared less.

Unless, that is, I was straight for a few hours. Then I was the most remorseful soul you'd ever want to meet. I was sorry, I was depressed, I was miserable, I was no good, I was guilty. I wanted forgiveness, I wanted God, I wanted rest, I wanted love, I wanted Gloria. And I wanted more drugs. Drugs were always available to the man with money, and that was one thing that was not in short supply.

My career could have skyrocketed right then, coming off three gold records and a monster hit like "Raindrops. . . ." But I hated myself, didn't consider myself worthy of fame somehow, and went about destroying myself for a reason that eluded me.

I recorded a song about the Lord that year called "Mighty Clouds of Joy." And I auditioned for the part of Jesus in the movie *Jesus Christ Superstar*. (I'm thankful now I didn't get that part, since the film was not honoring to God.) But those experiences kept the name of the Lord before me during my darkest days, and I think he had a hand in that. I knew somehow that God was interested in me and that the person I was really failing was him. If I could just get back to him, he was the way out. But I was too far gone. I just knew I was too far gone.

By now I was taking thousands and thousands of pills a month, sometimes five hundred on a weekend. I would be awake for days. I saw demons coming to eat me and I felt I could have any influence I wanted on the people around me . . . and often I could, seemingly talking anyone into anything.

I felt power. I felt like the devil, and more than one person told me I looked like the devil. There was a sinister force or person in control of me that had such power that I'm now convinced that Satan manifested himself in me many times. I would speak in a different voice and would see visions. I began to believe that drugs were the devil himself. It scared me to death, but I couldn't kick the pills.

They would throw me into high gear. My heart would race, and boy could I sing—just wide open for hours. I could do things on those highs that I couldn't do otherwise, or at least I had convinced myself so. But though every song sounded great to me, in truth they rarely were good.

A drug-infested mind and body becomes confused, and, man, that was me. I became paranoid and schizophrenic. I was one of the hottest acts in the country, but I was scared to go on stage without chemicals in my body. I didn't know if I could really sing or if people really liked me or if my records would keep selling or if I would be alive next week. I was crazy with fear and couldn't make the simplest decision, like whether or not to answer a ringing phone. I wouldn't go to see anybody, feared going to the grocery store with Gloria, didn't want to be on the street, and would sit in a cold sweat before I'd even answer the door.

I couldn't cope with seeing anybody. I couldn't drive and wouldn't even go to a movie. It was too much pressure. I knew it wasn't right and that surely I would have to die. A guy can't live like this.

I was wasted all the time, never once performing or recording without being high. I just couldn't do it. The recording sessions got tougher and tougher. The professionals didn't like having to start every song over again and again while the junkie tried to remember the lyrics or the melody or get his thing together. When I was singing right, I couldn't analyze it and duplicate it the next time.

I was in a fog, singing and hoping for the best. The drugs stood in the way of the talent the Lord gave me to pick up new songs quickly. I had often recorded a song after learning it an hour or so before, and do so now. I sure couldn't then.

Most of the time the hits I came out with were worth the wait, but it was an agonizing strain on everybody. Of the dozen or so songs on each album, ten would be mediocre and we would hit with one or two. With Chips producing, me singing the best I could, and with good material, we recorded at least one hit in every session. It was good for everybody else concerned, but for me . . . it just meant more money, and that meant more pills.

I slept when my body forced me to and I got up when it let me. I hit tremendous highs and lows every day, and I could hardly distinguish day from night. I couldn't remember what day it was or when the next gig was or when we had rehearsed last or when we were supposed to record. I didn't recognize people I should have known, and I had no memory for names or faces. I see people all the time now who remind me that they were in such and such recording session with me, but I haven't the foggiest recollection.

When I had my lows I knew I had to quit drugs or kill myself. Every binge of three or four days would leave my body in a state of wrecked exhaustion. And then would come the horror scenes. My body screamed for rest and a respite from the foreign substances and I felt as if I were about to explode. I wasn't drinking booze, but with Cokes and coffee and cigarettes, I was abusing my body with every known socially acceptable stimulant at my disposal.

Then I might make a fool of myself—go on a spending spree or collapse in public or walk off stage in the middle of a show. And then it was home to Gloria. Nothing she could say would please me and I'd make her stay awake and be with me on my high. At the smallest provocation —sometimes none at all—I flew into rages that lasted hours. I would rant and rave and scream, and if Gloria even once looked away or seemed bored, I punched her or pushed her down and beat her. My worst memories are of the pain I inflicted on my loved ones, and Gloria took as much as anybody. It is a miracle of God that she is with me today after two separations, a near divorce, and countless horror scenes.

I was in a profound state of depression every minute that I wasn't high. I awoke after every crash with great shame and humiliation for what I was doing to my family. I couldn't remember what I had said or done or whom I had attacked or what I had broken, but I knew I had done it again.

The enjoyment of the self-pity, though, was something I was never able to reconcile. It must have had something to do with the self-destructive nature that brought drug abuse into my life, but the hopeless feeling that it was all over for me had an ironic romance about it. It was crazy, I know, but I loved playing the wounded horse role and reveling in pity. Maybe it was a throwback to my dad's philosophy of life. I was living hard, and for sure I was headed for a young death. As for leaving a beautiful memory, I was failing.

Most of the time I was completely out of control. When I was attacking someone or smashing every breakable object in the house, inside I would be saying, *I wish I could stop! Why am I doing this?* Sometimes I would feel as if I were out of my body, watching the whole episode, observing and listening to a man I didn't even recognize. I was the feature attraction in the nightmare of the century and I wondered where it would all lead.

When a "friend" introduced me to cocaine, I figured, what's another drug? It seemed I had all I needed and wanted, but he said it was the ultimate sex trip. He was right. It was purely an aphrodisiac and it got me into a lot of trouble. It was a continuous thing too; you'd race for five minutes and then you'd want another snort. Now that it's behind me I can say that next to heroin—which I never tried—cocaine is probably the worst drug available today. It's a tool of the devil. He's got to be the author of drugs. God sure isn't.

I was having horror scenes like clockwork. I'd be on the wagon for a few days, then back on a binge, just like an alcoholic. I was into a vicious cycle of being famous and not being able to handle it, all the while thinking that because I was unable to handle it, I didn't deserve it.

At the peak of my career up to then, I was unable to take advantage of the fame or even enjoy it. It just made me more paranoid, put me under more pressure. I kept putting myself down. Being famous when I wasn't ready for it was just hell—worse than never having been famous at all.

Marriage to the only man she had ever loved had changed Gloria Thomas's life, but everything had quickly soured. She had hated being in New York, alone and pregnant, with B. J. gone most of the time. But she hated it worse when he returned and the horror scenes followed. She thought he had kicked drugs for a while when Paige was born, but it turned out he had simply quit taking them at home. Soon they were back in the house and he was irrational again.

"I knew it wasn't really B. J.," she says. "That's why I stayed. This person was not my husband. I feared him and I hated him and the life he had made for me, but I didn't hate B. J. I had to hang in and help beat the drugs and try to keep him alive. I so desperately wanted the old B. J. to return."

I believe that had Gloria not tried to take over, things would have been better, but I can't fault her for it now. No one would have said that I was fit to be the head of any household, especially one with a baby daughter and a young wife. But it bugged me continually to see her trying to salvage things and make them work. I was irrational, I know, but that was the effect it had upon me.

I could kick pills at home for a while, but as soon as I hit the road again I was right back into them. Gloria tried everything in her power to upset the pushers and the people around me who were using me. I hated her for it, yet I loved her for it. I fought her, but inside I was saying, "God, I hope you succeed." I was killing myself and I couldn't stop.

I had drugs hidden everywhere. When I wasn't taking them, I knew where they were.

Everybody thought Gloria was a fool to stay with B. J., but she was able to protect her daughter and she "just wanted him to stay alive, kick drugs and not ruin his life." It got to the point where she pleaded with his handlers to get help for him. She even appealed to their baser instincts. She knew the reasons they stayed close—it was for the money—so she tried to tell them that if he didn't get help, there would be no more B. J., thus no more money.

"I realize now I shouldn't have tried to wrestle the reins of the household from him, but I felt justified in doing the only thing I knew to do to help. It was only when I gave up trying to lead him that God put our marriage back together."

But there were years of torment to pay before that. Gloria set about trying to handle the business because she saw B. J.'s so-called associates ripping him off.

It hurt me terribly, but it was true. In a way I could hardly blame them. Here I was, a money-producing commodity, a guy with talent and marketability, but whom they could not respect as a person. I couldn't handle my personal life, so they probably reasoned that I didn't deserve all the money

I was making either. Slowly they began to rob me blind. Money was diverted into various expenditure accounts of which I had no knowledge. I didn't want to know. I trusted my people.

And I think at first they had good intentions. But no matter how much they might have admired my talent or loved me before, once that personal respect is gone, nothing goes right any more. This situation would eventually lead me into bankruptcy, but I never saw it coming.

They propped me up and sent me out to do a show or to record, and they tried to see to it that I made it there and back in one piece so the profit wouldn't be jeopardized, but never once did they really try to help until the money started to slack off. Then they recommended a psychiatrist.

I was willing to try anything. I had walked out of my second booking at the Copacabana in New York, and the owner threatened to have my legs broken. When I threatened to go to the newspapers, it got to be a really rank scene. Then I bought a house in the Connecticut countryside. It was quiet and peaceful, at least outside the house. Inside, the drugs flowed more freely and the horror scenes were more frequent.

Ironically, hit records and awards kept coming my way. In March of 1971 Houston held a B. J. Thomas Day after I had headlined at the annual Astrodome rodeo. They didn't know they were honoring the junkie of the year.

I was already in the category of addicts who are so far gone that only one in ten thousand ever kicks drugs. I wouldn't have given a nickel for my chances.

6   **wasted**

*By now, Gloria Thomas was shamelessly trying to stay in
the way of those she thought were trying to use B. J. "They
treated him like a piece of expensive luggage," she says.
"Put anything into it you want, but just don't scratch it."
She saw him manipulated, and she did some manipulating
of her own.*

   *She was forced to stay awake when he was high to
protect herself and to keep him from destroying their home.
When he finally slept every few days, she got busy*

searching for new ways to take pressure off him. It became her purpose in life, and his people called her The General behind her back.

She had told known pushers to stay away from her home. "If you come here, you will be busted; you have my word," she said. And when they whined that they had already given B. J. some stuff and needed to collect so they wouldn't get in trouble with their own supplier, she put on her most compassionate voice—thinking of what dope had done to her home—and said, "In every life, a little rain must fall." And she hung up.

Hours and hours were spent trying to keep B. J. calm, to bring him down after a horror scene. She would sit and cry with him for an hour, only to have a phone call or a visitor throw him back into a senseless rage. There was no harnessing the vicious animal the man became when he was irrational.

When he crashed he would tell Gloria that he was afraid. He felt like a crazy man and he couldn't control himself. He wanted to be normal and happy. "I never saw him cheerful in the morning for months on end," Gloria says. "He tried to smile, but his eyes were like tombstones. Half of him was dead, and to him total death would have been a blessing."

For a while the horror scenes were less frequent, maybe just a two- or three-day episode each month. That gave Gloria time to rest and regain her strength, preparing herself for the next scene and trying to get help. She didn't know where to turn.

"During those times between highs," she says, "B. J. was sensitive and kind and tender and affectionate. He was a loving father and enjoyed watching Paige grow. But things eventually grew worse than ever."

The bad times became so frequent and long that they overshadowed the good. B. J. had to take some time off from recording and touring because he couldn't work two nights in a row. The money slacked off, the mortgage was in trouble, Gloria had run out of ideas, and the associates were talking psychiatrist again.

The first thing the psychiatrist told me was that I could forget about getting right with God. He didn't want to put down my or anybody's religion, he told me, but it was not going to help in my case. I knew he was wrong, but I was hardly in a position to defend an argument, especially in favor of God.

Drugs were so much a part of me that I couldn't even keep from embarrassing myself on nationwide television. On *The Tonight Show,* Johnny Carson asked me how I could do so many one-nighters every year. "Well, I take a lot of drugs," I said. It wasn't funny and no one laughed.

"I know you didn't want to get into that," Carson told me later.

"No, I sure didn't. It just came out."

He had said before that I was one of the few singers that he felt he could really talk to on the show. Now he said he wouldn't have me on again unless I only sang. I vowed I'd never go back on television, and I didn't for about three

years. It's a wonder I didn't embarrass myself even more
that time with Johnny, I was so high.

My manager and agents landed me a part in a Western
movie called *Jory,* produced by Howard Menske—his first
after *Love Story.* It starred John Marley and Robbie Ben-
son, and I played a gunslinger who got bumped off in the
second reel. It was my first taste of acting, and I enjoyed it,
though the movie wasn't great and never did much. Worse,
being away from home for so long and my dad dying while
I was gone pushed me even more deeply into drugs.

I idolized Dad so much. I still believe that subconsciously
I emulated his somewhat self-destructive nature with my
devil-may-care attitude. If anything, I was worse off when
he was gone.

Johnny Carson was not the only personality I got into
trouble with during the drug years. When I first worked
with Burt Bacharach on "Raindrops Keep Fallin' on My
Head," I had laryngitis and had to have a doctor prescribe
something to shrink my vocal cords. It all worked out for
the best, obviously, but the next time we worked together,
there was trouble.

We were at the Century City Hotel in Hollywood, rehearsing the followup album to *Raindrops . . .* called
Everybody's Out of Town. The album would contain seven
new Bacharach songs, which are never easy to learn because the man is a sophisticated musical genius. I had been
working on them all day, but I was also high, and Burt
knew it.

He took little verbal shots at me all day in front of his

lyricist, Hal David, my conductor, and some others. I was getting a little steamed. He was being unfair because I was close to having each song down pretty well. But he was on my case because I was high. It had always seemed to me that he thought he was pretty hot stuff, though *Raindrops . . .* was only his first gold record, but now he was really getting to me.

About ten o'clock that night Burt came to the end of his patience with me. "B. J.," he said, "it's obvious you haven't worked very hard on these songs."

"Hey, I've been up since nine-thirty this morning workin' on 'em," I said.

"Well, I know you've been cutting in Memphis and maybe you're just not used to doing sophisticated music. Maybe this stuff is a little over your head."

I glared at him. "Look," I said, "I had million sellers before I ever saw you and I'll have 'em after you. I don't appreciate you saying something like that to me. I'll tell you what I'm gonna do, I'm gonna whip your tail." I made a move for him and he scampered off the piano bench, out the door, and down the hall. I didn't chase him; I just let him run.

"Oh, B., don't do that," Hal David said.

"That swine treats you the same way, Hal," I said. "Like he's the big star and nobody else is worth nothin'. I've taken enough off him."

I was sitting in my room later when my manager called. "Bacharach tells me you went crazy on him, B. Now what the—"

"Hey, don't go getting mad at me or you'll be lookin' for another job too," I said. "You better tell ol' Burt that he'd better call and apologize or I'll have the followup hit to *Raindrops* . . . myself. I don't care who wrote it, the followup will be mine. If he wants it to be one of his songs, he'll call me and apologize."

In my wildest dreams I never thought he'd call. But he did. A half hour later. "B. J.," he said, "I'm sorry I insulted you that way. I shouldn't have said it."

"ok," I said. "That's cool." We finished the session.

Frankly, if I had been him, I'd have told me to stick it. We cut another movie theme ("Long Ago Tomorrow") in San Diego a couple of years later, and when I walked into the session I asked Burt if I could talk with him. I wanted to apologize for having made such a fool of myself. "You don't have to say anything, B.," he said. "It's all right."

"No, I have to," I said. "Forgive me for what I did." We haven't been close since then, but we've both been quoted as saying nice things about each other. I always appreciated his attitude and I realized that I had been expecting too much from him. I wanted him not only to be a great musician but to befriend me and love me because that's what I thought I needed. Without being too hard on myself, I take the blame for what happened at Century City.

I'd like to work with Burt again someday if a project is just right for us. It would probably work best on a movie theme again though, since our styles are so different. I work on a thing slowly and try to keep a natural feel about it. He reads music and wants things done quickly and perfectly. But, anyway, I enjoyed working with him on *Raindrops . . . ,* and for sure it was my career hit up to then.

At home, Gloria was still trying to keep the show going, because her man was a drug addict and she thought he couldn't do it. But that just made things worse. The libbers can say what they want, but the woman is never going to be able to run a relationship like ours. If a man is alive and breathing, he's got to run it, or else it ain't gonna run right.

At the same time, I can't emphasize enough that I know why Gloria took over so much and tried to influence me. It became obvious that I responded to whatever person put the strongest influence on me or told me the most enticing story. Drugs confused me so that I just blew with the wind that seemed to be blowing hardest.

Gloria worked as hard as she could to show me she loved me. She took calls and tried to make decisions for me because she knew that if she left it with my manager or with Jerry or my lawyers, there was no tellin' what I might do. It bugged me, yet I was thankful, even though it just didn't work. That's not the natural order of things.

It still scares me to look back at the times I got so frustrated with what she was doing—and this would be heightened by the drugs, of course—that something or someone inside me wanted to kill her. Inside, I would say, "I'm going to pick her up and throw her right through that window." And I would have to refuse. I'd say, "I will not," and something inside would say, "Go ahead, do it."

"When I saw that look come over him, I ran like a scared rabbit," Gloria says. "I knew it wasn't even him. His forehead arched up and his eyes turned black as if there were no pupils. He talked in another voice and knew things I had done that no one could have told him because I had done them while he was asleep and had been with him all the time. It was demonic, I know now, but then I was sure that he was schizophrenic and had developed a whole other personality that wanted to kill me. It scared the life out of me."

Finally I knew that evil forces were at work in my body. They talked to me, especially when I was going through withdrawal, which I did many times. Once I lay on my bed and heard a voice curse me through the wall all day and all night. I never said a word for two days. The TV was on and I hallucinated that sportscaster Howard Cosell was talking to me. Later I recognized the voice in the wall as my own. I was sure I was going insane.

The voices suggested evil and criticized me constantly. The phrase "What a stupid idea" ran through my mind all the time. People who hallucinate on drugs think that they just took a little too much. I think not. I think they have opened themselves to demonic influence, and what they saw may not have been just a flashout; it may have been real. I believe the voices I heard were real.

One night on a tour I took a tremendous overdose of speed and got so high I couldn't even think. When I found myself grabbing another whole handful of pills, I realized they could kill me. In my stupor I prayed, "Oh, God, don't let them hurt me. Don't let me be high any more." He answered that prayer more specifically than I wanted. I simply didn't want to die from the overdose, but he also brought me completely down from my high. It was what I had asked for, but it wasn't what I really wanted. In the back of my mind, though, it convinced me that God was real.

I took almost all of 1973 off. "Rock and Roll Lullaby" was a hit and we had the money and time to do what we wanted. I almost even kicked drugs. They just didn't seem that important when I wasn't on the road all the time. We had four and a half acres of landscaped property around our house and it seemed we had dozens of people over every weekend.

Johnny Nash's band and my band would play, and there were week-long whiffle ball marathons. All we did was play outside and go to movies. Gloria and I would spend a weekend in New York, going to Madison Square Garden, eating out, and seeing every movie we wanted to see before we took a break.

Jerry didn't do drugs on the road so he could watch out for me. And I didn't do many drugs at home because everything was more relaxed. We had fun times, hilarious times, mellow and touching times. Things were good on the surface, and we began to really believe our hidden wishes and hopes that—just like when we were poor kids counting on a break—we would pull out of this too. We didn't have to be dead on drugs, we didn't have to lead miserable, horror-filled lives. There was a way out, and while we didn't talk about bad times during good times, we knew they still festered beneath the surface and that we'd have to deal with them soon.

When I wasn't doing drugs I was eating, and I gained about twenty-five pounds that year. We had a couple of horror scenes, and we smoked a lot of pot. But until I had to go on the road again to start more money coming in, we were almost straight. Nothing important had changed, but we had once again captured some temporary happiness and laughter. I dreaded the road, but eventually I had to return to it.

I was so high in New Mexico one night that my ears rang and I could hear my heart pounding and even the blood rushing through my veins. Antagonistic voices argued in my head and I couldn't get away from them. When I saw Indians galloping through the walls after me, I made the band pack up and head to another hotel at two in the morning. When we got to the new place, the hotel doctor gave me some sleeping pills and I popped eight or ten of them real quick and the voices went away.

When I got back, I told my shrink, "I hope you don't put me away, but this is what happened—" He said it was simply a form of withdrawal.

Because everyone thought I was really gone, I couldn't get the straight word from anybody but Jerry on the state of business or anything else. Even Gloria didn't think I could handle it. You get into a box just like Elvis was in before he died, where no one will say no to you. The main objectives of my road crew and my band, my lighting guy and sound guy—everybody—were to make me happy. They didn't set the stage or the system up for the drummer. They set it up for me. Everything I said or did was gold and whatever I wanted I got. I sure could have used some stark truth from somebody who cared, but as I've said, I'm not so sure it would have done any good by then anyway.

Anything at all that went wrong on the road made me mad and I was miserable. I chewed out my crew and sometimes even attacked them. When I wasn't happy, no one was happy. If I was in the mood, Jerry and I would walk through hotel lobbies just looking for tails to whip. Anybody that wasn't like us and seemed to be looking down his nose at us woke up the next morning wondering what in the world he had said or done and wishing he hadn't done it, whatever it was.

Then, because I was so high, I stayed mad when I got to my room. I might rant and rave all night about some little thing someone had done and how I'd like to kill him. I'd kick in the television set or even throw it out the window to the parking lot. More than once I left a hotel with a bill for as much as $8,000 in damages. I might curse a hotel operator and spend the night in jail after he or she called the police.

I was never the kind of a guy who could break a lot of rules without getting caught. It seemed as if I was paying for some stunt every time I turned around. When I came down and was straight for a few hours I was the first to feel ashamed and to apologize. But the straight hours were

becoming less and less frequent. I quit even trying to decide why I was doing what I was doing. Whole days and
nights were devoted to getting as high as humanly possible
and staying up as long as I could. Sometimes I went as long
as five days without sleep, sometimes without shutting up.

I hardly ever ate a decent meal. I looked like a skeleton:
a rich, well-dressed, dark, glassy-eyed bag of bones. Anyone
on dope could spot me a mile away. I gave new meaning to
the word *wasted*.

One morning in New York, after we'd been on the road
for two weeks and I had taken fifty or sixty pills a day, I
was crashing in bed, completely out. I was supposed to get
up and read for a part in the movie *The Lost Horizon*. I
couldn't even get up to get there and I lost the part, of
course.

Not long after that, the building we were staying in
caught fire. People were screaming through the halls, rac-
ing into the street, trying to salvage their belongings. Gloria
tried to wake me. "Don't bother me again until it gets to
the fifteenth floor," I told her. I wanted the extra sleep,
even if it might mean my life. We may have been the only
two people left in the building when the fire was finally
extinguished a few floors below us!

One of my strongest addictions was to Valium. I could
kick most anything for a few days, but not my Valium.
After I had gone to the psychiatrist for three years, he told
me that as far as he was concerned, I was fine. I knew then
that it was time to give up. If he was so shortsighted that
he couldn't tell that I was the same miserable person who

had walked into his office three years before, then there was nothing left for me to do. I began to overdose on pills every other day or so. My lips and nails turned blue and I gagged on my own vomit as my body tried to reject the foreign substances. I was so dead to the world that even that didn't wake me.

Gloria had to check me every fifteen minutes, just to make sure I was breathing. Often I wasn't and she had to revive me. I knew that when she finally had her fill and would quit loving me enough to do that, I was going to be in big trouble. I dreaded that day, and it was not far off.

7   **alone**

"I had made excuses for B. J. all along," Gloria says. "I blamed it on his instant popularity and the fact that no one treated him like a real person. He was a personality and no one gave him credit for having a brain. Everywhere he even walked was valuable.

"There were unbelievable demands upon his time. Even without drugs that kind of pressure could drive a person crazy. You're dead tired all the time and you need to get your head together or you'll lose it. Everybody loves you,

based solely on your last performance, and you know it. If you do well, they love you. If you don't, or if you get in trouble and make a fool of yourself or get strung out on drugs and your income drops, you're a bum and they abandon you.

"Only two or three people stuck with B. J. through the highs and lows, and I wasn't one of them. B. J. says that I never let him down, and that's basically true, but the day came when I had had enough. I ran out of ideas and compassion. I was so exhausted that he once misfired a .44 caliber pistol in our bedroom and I didn't even stir.

"Besides that, he was tired of my trying to handle his affairs. There were too many people around to suit me. Family, hangers-on, roadies, associates—everybody had more of B. J. than I did and they all enjoyed taking credit for everything he did right. No one would take any responsibility for the fact that he was killing himself on drugs."

Gloria was still trying to run things and it was really starting to hack me off. I could see that she wasn't really making any business decisions—she just thought she was. She assumed she was handling a lot of things, but she was just being patronized by my people. She would "handle" something while I was sleeping off a binge, and then when I got up I'd head to the office and handle it myself. It caused a lot of trouble between us, but I know now—and down deep I knew then—that she was doing it with the best of motives. She loved me and she hated what I was doing to myself, what my people were allowing me to do to myself, and most of all, what they themselves were doing to me.

Gloria thinks B. J. knew she was planning to leave and that he subconsciously tried to make things harder for her so she wouldn't prolong the agony. She had hoped to help make him well, but when her love turned to disgust, she had to leave. She had hung in with him for several years, taking pills herself at times just to stay up with him.

She had received Christ as a ten-year-old but had not ever become a consistent churchgoer or Christian. During the time she and B. J. lived in Connecticut, she went to a different church almost every week. She went forward at almost every service, seeking to receive Christ again and again, never once hearing how to live for him or how to apply biblical principles to her life. All she knew was that she didn't measure up and that she had little to go on, even after pleading with God for help week after week. At one point she prayed and asked God to do whatever he had to do to rescue B. J. from death.

She prayed, "Please help me. Please save me. Please show me a way out." She tried telling B. J. that God was the answer, but after a while she wasn't so sure herself. The harder things got, the more B. J. turned to drugs, and the more drugs he did, the harder things got. Nothing seemed to work with him, and Gloria knew she had to get out. She would take her daughter and go back to Texas.

She had become an insomniac. There was no peace and rest and no longer any way to deal with the daily crises. Her body was run down and she worried that her mind

*might be going too. When she finally decided to leave, she
slept soundly for the first time in months. One day in July
of 1974, she packed bags for herself and Paige and drove
to the airport. On her way out the door, B. J. asked, "What's
wrong?"*

*"I lived in an apartment in Fort Worth for five months
without missing him. After the first two weeks of depression, I started dating. I kicked up my heels and lived
it up."*

*Paige, however, was not happy. She was too young to
know all that had gone wrong. All she knew was that her
daddy was no longer around. And when Gloria took her to
her first day of school, Paige held her mother's leg and
pleaded, "Mommy, you can't leave me!" until both were
in tears. She held on as if her life depended on it until the
teacher pulled them apart.*

*For the first time in as long as she could remember,
Gloria Thomas was not worrying about the future. She was
not even thinking about it. She was enjoying the present.
It wasn't extravagant, living on a modest check that B. J.'s
people sent each week, as opposed to the thousands and
thousands and thousands of dollars that had been at her
disposal in the past.*

*She had to pay rent, keep Paige fed, clothed, and in
school, buy a car, and watch her budget. It was a new
experience.*

Of course I had known it was coming, but when she was
all of a sudden dressed and packed and on her way out the
door that day, it hurt me deeply. She and Paige were the

only things in the world that I really cared about, but I hadn't even said so for ages. I had been treating Gloria bad for so long I hardly knew another way to live. We had always fought over her trying to run things, so I guess she figured it would please me if she butted out. It didn't. Even with all the people running in and out of that house in the countryside, I was lonelier than I had ever been. Now there was no one to come home to. I went through five dark months, and even though she and I often talked by phone, the love was gone—or so it seemed.

By Christmastime I couldn't stand it any more. I wanted so badly to quit doing drugs and to get back with Gloria that I left Connecticut for Texas. We had a love reunion and I asked her to take me back. She agreed. We moved out to a beach house outside Forth Worth and I tried like everything to kick pills. When I lapsed into epileptic seizures, a brain tumor was incorrectly diagnosed. It appeared for a while that I would have to have brain surgery because of what I had done to myself with drugs. That was almost too much for Gloria to take. Even with the operation, I could be a zombie. Later we found out that my Valium addiction had caused the seizures, a symptom of withdrawal. I thought I had ruined my brain with drugs and had turned myself into an epileptic.

Gloria is a strong woman, but all the years I had put her through by then had softened her a bit. She was no longer the tough girl who wouldn't cry. She was trying to hold things together; I was resenting her for it; and we both wound up mental cases. There were days when she fought me physically to keep me from my pills. Johnny

Cash says his wife, June, did the same thing. Isn't that some picture?—June Carter rasslin' that big hunk of a guy? I'm bigger than Gloria too, but she punched me out once. Gave me a black eye and really got my attention.

Unfortunately, when I hit her it got my attention too. I slugged her once during 1974 and broke her nose and wrenched her neck. Then I couldn't look at her. Even when the facial bruise went away the neck pain remained. Every time I saw her I wanted to kill myself. I felt so guilty that I started to resent her for it. I was being typically irrational, but it was as if the pain was there for all the world to see what I had done to her.

We moved into a house in Fort Worth, but I couldn't stand to be around Gloria any more. The whole mess was my fault and I had given her a rotten life, but somehow I felt as if I was the one who needed an escape. Each day was one big guilt trip. The next time I left Fort Worth, I knew I would not be coming back. I called Gloria a couple of weeks later. "I won't be coming home," I said.

Gloria reacted simply. "Fine," she said, and almost immediately filed for a divorce. They had been together for nearly a year since the first separation, yet it had been ten times worse than the first nightmarish year of their marriage. B. J. was as heavily into cocaine as speed by now, and he seemed to do drugs twenty-four hours a day. She had traveled with him on almost every road tour, leaving Paige with the maid. Her whole purpose seemed to be to keep him straight.

Every trip found Gloria either abandoned somewhere or

angrily sent home early. There were horror scenes nearly every day. She was left on her own in Mexico; B. J. kicked her out of Brazil; he beat her up on Christmas Eve. Like clockwork, he would call a few days later, crying and begging to come home. She always let him. There was always hope. Whenever he was broken and remorseful, she saw light at the end of the tunnel. She couldn't give up. She just couldn't make the decision. During one of his worst low spells, B. J. cut what was to become one of his best sellers, "(Hey, Won't You Play) Another Somebody Done Somebody Wrong Song," *but he was so mentally and emotionally wounded by then that he couldn't enjoy it.*

Gloria had been admitted to the hospital three different times during the year, mostly from exhaustion. Paige was hurting and sad, and everyone, even B. J., seemed to hate Gloria.

At long last she had become cold and indifferent. She would take care of B. J., but she found it hard to love him even when he was straight. At times she hated him and his irresponsibility. When he passed out, it took her hours to drag him to bed, being careful to maintain what little was left of his dignity.

Everyone advised her to leave him, but she had done that before and had wanted him back. When she returned to Fort Worth after attending her younger sister's funeral— her mysterious death had been a terrible shock to Gloria— B. J. had gone to California. She didn't care.

When he called a few days later and asked her to meet him in Nashville, she felt the old familiar tug. She went to

*him. They spent a weekend in a motel room, straight and
in love. But when she went out on an errand, he was crazy
again when she returned. She endured another horror scene,
but it was the last straw. She knew her love had been
snuffed out. She returned to Fort Worth. When B. J.
called to say he wasn't coming home, she felt free. It was
not yet summer, 1975.*

By now Don Perry was helping manage me and the members of the band and I were so into cocaine it was unbelievable. We spilled more coke across this country than most junkies will use in a lifetime. They tried to stay up with me, but they couldn't. Nobody could. I made mental basket cases of everybody around me because I could always do twice as much dope as they could. Even long-time addicts were amazed that they could never stay with me in consumption. It's a wonder I'm still alive, considering how many times my bodily functions quit and someone had to revive me.

I didn't know what was happening to Gloria, and I didn't care. I had deserted her. Everything about her made me feel guilty and I didn't want to think about it. I was so far past being responsible that there was no word to describe me, though I'm sure she tried a few.

*As hard as she tried to fill up her life with other things
and other people, Gloria could not forget B. J. It wasn't that
she missed him or even had a glimmer of anything more
than pity for him, but the reality of her own situation*

stared her in the face every day and reminded her that he was responsible. It would lead to serious emotional and mental crises, but for now her worries were practical ones.

Counting on the usual check from B. J.'s New York people to cover her bank account, she had written and mailed out $2,500 worth of checks to pay household bills. It never arrived. She was overdrawn by more than two thousand dollars, couldn't pay the rent, and was about to endure more traumas in a few months than most people face in a lifetime.

8   **death**

I may have been high most of the time, but I wasn't stupid. It didn't take me long to realize that two of the guys from New York who had signed to manage me were going to take my money for as long as I lasted. Trouble was, Don Perry began to like me. He was basically a good guy and couldn't stand doing a number on me once he got to know me and saw the problems I had.

We became close friends and he began letting me have some of my money rather than funneling all of it to the

New York cronies. He got in a lot of legal trouble for that, but he was trying to show me that, "Hey, maybe those guys are trying to screw you, but I'm not."

I traveled with him, but even with a friend and a hit ("Wrong Song"), I knew I was headed nowhere. My mind was clouding over and the world looked black. I was featured as the Country Artist of the Week in *Cashbox*'s Country News column once in 1975. The photo showed a mean, cool-lookin' dude wearing shades, long curly hair framing an empty face of stone.

Chips Moman produced the followup to "Wrong Song" for me, an album we cut in Nashville with songs like "Help Me Make It to My Rocking Chair," "Ballyhoo Days," and "Goodtime Charlie's Got the Blues." I was high the whole time, so Chips and I were at each other constantly. We are, I believe, of similar talent levels, but I was so out of it that he couldn't respect me. After laboring for hours to get a song down right, he would just as soon have punched me as look at me. The big blowup came, however, over money.

I had planned to take some time off after recording and had asked Chips if he could loan me five thousand dollars when the taping was finished. He said sure. At least that's the way I remembered it.

When I asked him for it later, he said, "I told you I'd give it to you when the record company paid me."

"You're a liar," I said. "That's not what you told me at all!" He insisted that it was and I stormed off to a party to get ripped. I snorted up several thousand dollars worth of cocaine and was finally so high that I really began big-mouthing. "I'm gonna get my money off that sucker," I announced.

Everybody else was mellow and nearly asleep. "No, man," they said, "you don't want no trouble. Don't do that. It's not worth it." But when most everyone had either drifted off or split, I was still up rockin'.

"I'm goin' to get my money," I said.

When I arrived at the studio, Chips was just about to leave. "Man, I really need some money," I said. "Can you give me that five thousand?"

"I don't have it."

"Well, then can you give me a grand?"

"B. J., I ain't got it, man."

"Can you give me five hundred?"

"I don't have it."

"Chips," I said, "when you tell me you don't have five thousand dollars, I can believe you. And when you tell me you don't have a thousand, I can believe that. But when you tell me that you don't have five hundred, I don't believe that."

"Don't call me a liar!"

I pulled out my hunting knife with its six-inch blade. "Hey," I said, "I'll call you anything I want to, and if you don't like it, then maybe I'll stick ol' Uncle Henry here in you. Me and Uncle Henry, we gon' do whatever we want."

He spun away from me and over to his golf bag, but as he yanked out a club and turned around, I was upon him, the point of my knife resting on his chest. "You even think about hitting me with that club," I said, "and I'll kill you." My glazed eyes dared him.

One of his flunkies grabbed another club and came up behind me. "Chips, you'd better tell this guy that if I so much as hear his shirt rustle, I'm gonna put this thing right through you." I meant it and they could tell. They dropped their clubs and backed away. I know I would have killed him, and it horrifies me to think about it even now. The Bible says that I committed murder in my heart.

For some reason, Chips didn't hold it against me. He knew the drugs really had me and that I wasn't myself. A few months later he called and suggested that we get together and cut some more songs. I couldn't understand his compassion, but it sure said something to me about the kind of a man he is. It was two years before we got back together on a project, and by then it was an entirely different scene in the very same studio [see Preface].

Looking back, I remember that the knife and the drugs strangely made me feel like a man, but I didn't like the man they had made of me. I could never be that guy again, and I would never want to be, though I confess there are parts of him that I miss. He was always trying to keep up the game. Very often, that old B. J. Thomas was fun-loving. There was nothing he couldn't or wouldn't do. Someone might warn against doing something and he would say, "Hey, it's us, man. We can do anything we want!" He was a big-hearted guy too, one that gave away thousands of dollars to good causes. The problem with that B. J. was that he didn't have Christ in his heart. He was spiritually bankrupt.

I was an ironically romantic figure then, but basically life was a depressing, hell-raising, horror-filled existence. I'd been on drugs for almost nine years and had nothing to look forward to except dropping dead. Whenever I blew it and took an overdose, I just sat around waiting and wondering if it would be the one that would do me in. I took forty pills just a few minutes after taking fifty and figured, who cares? I nearly died many times, but the Lord refused to let me go. That's the only explanation.

I began to take more drugs than even I thought I was capable of doing. If and when I allowed myself to think, I realized that I had ruined and lost my family, the one thing in the world that I loved. But I wouldn't even send them money; I was that calloused. And I wasn't about to leave Gloria my $22,000 Mercedes either, so I had someone drive it off for me one night. I didn't know or care what she was supposed to do for a car then.

Gloria was losing her mind. Her life had fallen apart and she found she had no reserves, nothing to fall back on. Hilarious laughter rang in her head and voices tortured her for days. She called some friends and talked very slowly and deliberately, afraid she would crack at any moment. "If you don't bring me something to knock me out," she said, "you're going to have to take me somewhere. I'm losing it."

She hadn't slept for more than a few minutes in three

days. Bill collectors called for their money. The bank
called. Don and others of B. J.'s people called. What was
she supposed to do with no money? Pack up and go nurse
B. J. at his rented mansion in California? The gall of their
even asking! They should have been sending money or a
car. She was through with B. J. And she told the bank to
either come and put her in jail or quit calling. "There is
nothing I can do."

Her friends brought a drug that allowed her to sleep
for a few hours, and when she awakened, she was able to
hold on a little longer. Shortly thereafter she received
another shock, one that would test her feelings about B. J.
It was a call from Don about near tragedy in Hawaii.

Just before our flight over there where I was supposed to
sing at an army base, I took eighty pills. By the time I got
on stage I was so high and dried out that I couldn't sing a
note. I asked the audience to forgive me and told them I
was sick. I threw my hat into the crowd and received a
standing ovation—I suppose for my honesty. It wasn't honesty at all.

I drove all around the island that night looking for some
cocaine, but I couldn't score any anywhere. We were going
to fly to another island in the morning, but when I got
back to my room near dawn, I started coming down from
my high. I thought I would die. "Whoever's packin' my
clothes had better get started and get me to the plane because I can't move," I said.

They tell me I was still conscious when we got to the plane, but I don't remember anything about it. Somehow they got me into the seat and fastened the belt before I lapsed into a deep, deep sleep. From the incredible eighty-pill high, I was suffering a crash that was more than any body could take, especially mine. When my friends realized that I seemed to have quit breathing, they stuck a compact mirror under my nose. No sign of breath. My lips and finger nails turned blue and then black. I was given oxygen, but for all practical purposes, I had died. Everyone was sure of it because I didn't seem to respond even to the oxygen. As we landed on the big island, an ambulance met the plane and rushed me to a Catholic hospital.

When I woke up the next day I asked how close a call it had been. "You were gone," someone said. "For almost two hours you were hooked up to machines that did your breathing for you."

I told a visiting nun, "I don't know why I made it, Sister. I didn't really care to and I don't know what I'm going to do now."

She asked me to bow my head, and she prayed a beautiful prayer, asking God to show me why he had spared my life and that he had a purpose for me. I believed that it was true that God cared about me, but I didn't know where to turn next. The only thing I knew was coke and speed, and I had three prescriptions for uppers in my pockets. Before I left the hospital, the pharmacy filled my prescriptions. My friends were sure I had learned my lesson, but within a few days, I secretly popped so many uppers that I was hooked again.

I had fallen into a speed trap. I would take eight uppers and need sixteen to duplicate the high once I started coming down. And when I came down from the sixteen, I would need thirty-two, then sixty-four. My body and mind were wasting away. I couldn't even think, and when I could talk, I'd call Gloria.

I wanted to tell her that I loved her and missed her and wanted to come home to her, but I was met with coolness and wound up telling her that I hated her.

Back in Houston the dog had been stolen, the car had disappeared and Gloria was being careful about security. One night, while Paige had a friend sleeping over, Gloria went to doublecheck the front door lock. She awoke several hours later in a pool of her own blood from a blow to the head. Police theorized that a burglar had been scared by her, hit her and thought he had killed her, and ran off.

She was stitched up and released, but she was soon forced to move for being unable to pay the rent. She held a garage sale to raise money. The car that B. J.'s people finally rented for her had starter problems and was towed in for repairs. Five months after he had left her, B. J. began sending a little money now and then. Had he come to his senses?

No, I still fully intended to let our divorce go through. Jerry had taken some time off from traveling with me and was taking care of our mother in East Bernard, Texas. I

Six Flags Over Texas, Summer 1977: B. J., with Frank Edmond-son, Contemporary Product Coordinator for WORD Records, holds award recognizing *Home Where I Belong,* the first gospel album ever to go to #1 its first month on the National Religious Bestsellers list. The album remained in #1 spot for almost a year.

"For ten years I had captive audiences and nothing to say. Now . . . people learn quickly where I'm coming from and where I stand." Above: Autograph session, Dallas, 1977. Below: Press conference, Atlanta, 1977.

"Would the Lord want me to shoot for mediocrity? As long as he has called me to serve him, I owe him my best effort." Here B. J. receives 1978 Grammy award for "Best Inspirational Performance" with his album *Home Where I Belong.* (Wm. R. Eastabrook photo)

"Some day soon I have to quit traveling. . . ."
For the 1978–79 school year B. J. and Gloria are
taking Paige out of school and hiring a tutor to travel
with them so they can all be together.

On release of first gospel album *Home Where I Belong*, WORD, Inc. honored B. J. with April 1977 Dallas reception. Happy people, left to right: Stan Moser, Vice President, Marketing; Roland Lundy, National Sales Manager, Records and Music; WORD recording star Evie Tornquist; B. J.; Dan Johnson, Director, Marketing and Promotion, Records.

Reception at Universal City Hotel in Universal City, California, introduces album *Home Where I Belong* to Los Angeles area bookstore dealers and media. Here, after having given testimony for the first time, B. J. chats with Dr. Stanley Mooneyham, President of World Vision International.

Billy Graham Crusade, Las Vegas, Nevada, 1978.
B. J. at microphone. (All Crusade photos on these two pages
courtesy of Russ Busby)

Cliff Barrows (far right) confers with Billy Graham
as (right to left) Johnny Cash, June Carter Cash, B. J.,
and Don Perry look on.

"The best way
I know to share
my testimony is
to sing it."
—B. J. Thomas.

Left to right, below: B. J. Thomas, June Carter Cash,
Johnny Cash, Billy Graham, and George Beverly Shea.

Home where we belong.
(Phil Van Duivendyk photo)

begged him to come back on the road with me. I had nothing and no one and I wasn't even treating Don like a friend very often. With no family near and few friends, I needed Jerry with me. It was as if I didn't want to die alone. And I wasn't sure death was going to be very far off.

9  answers

Gloria had tried in every way she knew to depend upon the Lord. When it didn't seem to work, she decided there was no God. There was no help. More than anything, she changed her mind about B. J. He was not a nice man who had just had a lot of bad things happen to him. No, he was what he was and he was what he did. After all the years of not really believing that B. J. wanted to hurt her, she had no other choice now. "His daughter and I were starving to death while he was flying all over the country.

"Jim and Micah Reeves, a couple I had met a year before, did everything they could to help. Jim was a rodeo worker and Paige took to him like the desperate little fatherless girl that she was. He took her for walks while Micah told me about Christ. They loaned me a car and neighbors brought me food, but I rejected their witness. Somehow I got moved into an apartment, but I was fast losing my equilibrium.

"I screamed at Paige, lashing out at her if she asked even a simple question. And I couldn't make decisions."

For the girl who had always been self-sufficient, it was humiliating to sit at her bathroom mirror in the morning and find herself still sitting there in the afternoon when Paige returned from school. She had used up her strength, her energy, her everything. She was—simply—out of it. She was just twenty-six years old and she feared she wasn't going to survive.

Missionary candidates named the Womachs moved in across the driveway and befriended Paige. The husband counseled Gloria when she came to the end of herself. Once she had begun crying and couldn't stop for twelve hours. Mr. Womach gave her projects, things to accomplish each day. Take a walk, he said. Do your household chores by a certain time. Put on your makeup in the morning. It helped. And he and his wife witnessed in their own quiet way.

B. J. visited Gloria in the fall, painting a fantasy picture of Hawaii and asking her to go there and live with him in paradise. No work, just play—golf every day and a life of

*ease. There was no way in the world to do what he talked
about, but in her irrational state, Gloria said sure, why not,
I'll go. He would pick her up soon.*

   *But when he left, she started crying again and couldn't
stop. Mr. Womach talked with her for six hours, convincing
her that the last thing in the world she needed—especially
right then—was to go back with an insane drug addict.
"There wasn't a chance that I could survive it again after
all we'd been through and the times we had tried. I called
B. J. and told him I wasn't going with him."*

   *Gloria was a physical and mental wreck, but she tried
strengthening herself by resting, not going out, not even
answering the phone. She invested all her time in Paige.
"I took care of her and fed her and dressed her and got her
to school and tried to love her and give her the stability
she hadn't had for years. I even quit screaming at her."*

   *Though she had decided there was no God, something
about the way Jim and Micah talked to her drew her back
to them. The thoughtful missionaries across the way and
Jim and Micah's always being available seemed the only
bright spots in her life. But even those lights were blotted
out when Gloria suffered her scariest, most revealing
experience with deep depression in December 1975.*

   *All the struggling and seeking and working and
enduring, she decided, had been for nothing. All hope
for the future was gone. Life was meaningless and sleep
brought nightmares. She dreamed of being trapped in holes
by wicked beings, but even more dreadful was the prospect
of waking up and having to face another day. It was more*

than she could bear. She lost gaps of hours again and again, and when it became dark suddenly, she couldn't tell if it was dawn or dusk.

When she realized that nothing in the world she could think of would make her happy, she wasn't sure she wanted to live any more. She tried to imagine being anyone or having anything she wanted—even the old, straight B. J.— and she knew in her heart that even that wouldn't make her happy. She didn't want to be rich, married, or anything. Her problem was deeper than a lack of love or companionship. She wanted to be dead, and that—she thought—was a problem with only one solution.

But there was one tiny glimmer. When she wasn't thinking about the "freedom" of death, she was thinking of a million and one questions for Jim and Micah. Finally, she began asking them.

For the first time in her life, Gloria's questions seemed to have answers, answers straight from the Bible. How am I supposed to react to such a husband? Was I wrong in filing for divorce? Should I have stayed with him? What can I do next? Does God care?

"They answered me with God's principles, documented from Scripture. Even when it seemed ridiculous, there it was in the Bible. And my 'logical' methods certainly hadn't worked."

Even more importantly, she received answers and counsel about her own spiritual status with God. As a child she had been led to understand that "if you did this you were this kind of a person and if you did that you were that kind

*of a person. God was a faraway Person who came to me in
a little Book I couldn't understand. All I knew was that I
was supposed to be good, whatever that meant. I was taught
no principles, and half the time I felt like a bad girl
without knowing why. I believe I asked Jesus to come into
my heart as a child. That made an eternal difference, but
my life wasn't transformed until years later when I finally
decided to live by God's principles on faith.*

*"For once the emphasis was not on being either a good
girl or a bad girl but on developing a relationship with
Jesus Christ. Finally, I had received some teaching on how
to live by God's standards. Life wasn't a cruel joke on me.
There was a way to attain complete happiness and peace
regardless of circumstances. There had to be a way, and I
was going to find it."*

*She talked with Jim and Micah at their home in Hurst,
Texas, several evenings until very late. Finally, it was as if a
light went on in her head. She began to see that God was
not a cosmic supreme being who cared only that a person
was good or bad. She saw him as a Person who loved her
and cared about her and wanted her as a friend. He wanted
her happy and forgiven.*

*"I had always thought that God had done what he was
supposed to do and that the rest was up to me. It was news
to me that he had any responsibility any more. It was his
responsibility to take my worries. Here was a God who
would not let me go, no matter what. He was going to
look after me for the rest of my life. Nothing could separate*

*me from his love, the Bible said. And no one can pluck
me out of his hand. What glorious truth and freedom!"*

*It became obvious to Gloria why she had been forced
through such turmoil, and she even began to see why B. J.
had resented her so. Their marriage had not been based
on God's principles. To her, the Bible said that she should
have supported B. J. no matter what kind of man he was—
not endorsing his lifestyle, but not hassling him, nagging
him, running his business and his life. Her job was to help
him and stay with him and submit to him. She knew all
the reasons that sounded ridiculous. He could be dangerous
to her and her daughter. But would he if she didn't cross
him? Could she win him over with the love of God?*

*Whether or not it would work, she didn't know. As
always, she was willing to try anything. She had always
been so self-sufficient. Little Miss Get It Done. Little Miss
Handle It. Her will had needed breaking and she had
needed to see her own weaknesses. That was what the past
few months had all been about. But she was ready for God
now. There was nothing left of her old self.*

*Without telling Jim or Micah of her intentions, she drove
home, telling herself, "All right, you're going to try it.
You're going to see what happens. Even though you've been
down the aisle of more than a hundred churches trying to
get saved and/or recommitted, you're going to give God a
chance again."*

*It shocked her that this decision was so attractive after
all her similar attempts had failed. But there was something*

different about this. It wasn't religion. It wasn't trying. It was dying. It was letting God do it. What an oasis! If this doesn't work, she thought, there truly is no hope.

She knelt alone by her bed and prayed for an hour, giving God everything that came to her mind. She gave him B. J., she gave him her pride, her situation, her daughter. "I could feel the room literally filling up. My shoulders quit aching and seemed to rise three inches. I gave God the future, the drugs, the fear, the depression, my heart, my pain, my loneliness, everything.

"When I was finished and stood I just grinned, loving God so much that I couldn't think of anything else. It gave me an unbelievable courage, unlike anything I ever felt before. I didn't know how much to hope for with B. J. and me, but I knew that my relationship with God had just begun. And it was right."

It was a couple of days after Christmas, 1975.

I was scheduled to play Houston's Astro Hall with Neil Sedaka on New Year's Eve and three days at a California amusement park a few days later, so I tried to stay fairly straight for about nine days beforehand. Otherwise I wouldn't have been able to work more than three days straight because I would be awake the whole time and have to crash after the third day.

People have said that they find it hard to believe that I spent three thousand dollars a week on dope, but ask Greg Allman how much he spent on coke when he was really into it. I'll bet it was twice that much. I was paying between twenty-two and twenty-three hundred dollars an ounce for some pretty heavy coke, and most of the time, from 1974 on, I was doing two ounces a week.

I know that sounds like a lot, but I was so into it that a gram snorted up one nostril wouldn't even wake me up. I had to snort six or seven grams up each side to get a hit. Two ounces in seven days? Often.

Money was no object. Dope was my career. The singing was simply a means to an end. The better money we made, the more drugs we could do. Score with a hit record? Super. That sets us up on dope for a year or two. Everything else was a sideline. I got such a low self-image that I felt terrible twenty-four hours a day. I didn't even sleep soundly. When I crashed I had nightmares, and while my body may have been immovable, my mind raced.

A song we recently recorded for my new gospel album *Happy Man* has a line in it that says it all: "Lost and feelin' lonely had become ordinary; I was always glad to see another day go by." How true. Sundown meant we'd made another day. That was all.

I arrived in Houston December 28 and my friends threw an all-night drug party for me. Pot, speed, downers, cocaine —everything flowed more freely than I had ever seen. Suddenly, here was all I wanted and more. Boy, I got wasted. I mean, I really got tore up.

It was the wildest high I had ever been on, and it's a wonder I didn't go out with a bang. I was just roaring, flying, my body in a frenzied fit. I was awake all night and all the next day and right on through the New Year's Eve show. Somehow I got through that, my body screaming for rest and my mind begging for more coke and pills. I kept slugging them down. There was no standing still, no rest. Hardly any thinking. In the back of my mind I knew that the next handful of pills or snort of coke could be my last, but I didn't care. I had passed the point of all reason and nearly the point of no return, so I figured I might as well get it over with, enjoy it while it lasted and go blazing off into eternal oblivion.

I did uppers and coke for days, not sleeping a minute, even on the plane back to California. I paced, I talked, I laughed, I fidgeted, I smoked cigarettes, I drank Cokes— anything, everything but relax. I couldn't come down and I didn't want to, though my body was rebelling.

I was sick and my remedy was more coke, more pills, more grass. I was on a toboggan slide to hell and I was gonna find out just how much this ol' body could take. I was too wasted to even wonder if anyone had ever done so many drugs in so few days or stayed up for as long as I had. I was inhuman.

At the amusement park on the second, third, and fourth of January I cursed the owner from the stage for making me fulfill my contract when I was "sick." It was always somebody else's fault. I could hardly sing, and I told the people that I didn't care. It was an embarrassing farce.

No other jobs were lined up because my reputation had spread. My managers didn't think I'd be able to continue performing for long anyway so they were afraid to book anything too far ahead of time.

Here it was the fourth of January and I had been awake since December 28 with no sign of slowing down.

No one could talk to me. They looked at me with pity and I hated them for it. Jerry and my road manager and I went back to the house I was renting for a thousand dollars a month in Pacific Palisades. It was a beautiful place, but I couldn't enjoy it. It was wide open with lots of windows, a pool table, and no help. It was hard to find servants who were drug addicts, and that's what I needed: someone to take drugs with me.

By the sixth of January, I was a walking corpse. There was no way I could continue without sleep, and as I began to crash I became violent. I almost attacked anyone who even looked upon me with love and concern. The people who cared about me were in danger for their lives. My life was jeopardized too. Don discovered me standing on one of the walls that surround the house, overlooking a 100-foot sloping drop to the ocean. I hadn't planned to commit suicide; I had simply found myself there. I began to think about the peace and pleasure of ending it all, but Don talked me down.

After having been high and awake for eleven straight days, I finally collapsed in total exhaustion. When I awoke, I didn't know if it was day or night. All I could remember was having wanted to attack and kill Jerry. I cried and begged forgiveness and promised him I would never touch cocaine again. I meant it with all my heart.

But my heart did not rule my body. My mind and will ruled it, and they had long since been surrendered to dope.

A few days later a guy came to buy some pot from me. I took a couple of hits of his cocaine and my vow went right out the window. The crazy thing was, it didn't make me high. I had burned myself out. For the next two weeks I sat around the house with the guys, going through a couple of pounds of marijuana, smoking all day long. I was at rock bottom, the most miserable I had ever been. I had no highs, no lows. I couldn't relax enough to play cards, so I shot pool for hours. There was nothing to plan for, nothing to enjoy. I snorted cocaine and nothing happened. I smoked dope and nothing happened. I took Valium and didn't even mellow out.

I slept for only a few minutes at a time, so I began going to bed at the same time every night, regardless of how I felt. It didn't help. Even my emotions were ambiguous. I was no longer angry. I was not into self-pity. I simply had a great, deep sense of frustration and emptiness. *Tonight I'll lie down and tomorrow I'll get up.* There was no hope for anything else.

Nights were blacker than nights should be, and I don't remember one ray of sunshine, though January days in the Palisades are always bright. It was a month of gloom and darkness, of monstrous clouds. I was as close to the valley of the shadow of death as I ever want to be without dying.

We rarely ate. Every few days I tried having eggs for breakfast, but my appetite was gone. I did twenty joints a day from my unlimited supply, and all it did was give me the feeling that I was in a vacuum. Nothing was happening. I was living death.

I had a very real sense that the next cocaine binge would be my last. My professional life was over. No gigs were planned; everything was off. People were saying, "Don't book him—he's flipped out." Absolutely no one would book a drug addict. Don tried to talk to me about some business but I was so abusive that he left in tears.

I called Gloria a couple of times just to hear her voice. Suddenly, strangely, she sounded more beautiful and at peace than I had ever heard her. Ever.

10   home

In the past, when I had called Gloria, I had always been met with coolness. If I asked her how she was, she would say, "Fine. As fine as any mother and daughter could be whose husband and father had deserted them." Her self-sufficiency had robbed me of any sensitivity to her need.

She had even been cold a few months before when I had kept Paige for a few days and took her to Disneyland. She never allowed any door of hope to the future to even crack open slightly. Even Paige was stronger than I was.

She talked about the Lord often and what she was learning at her Christian school. I envied her, and I missed them both and wanted them back. But I wouldn't admit it.

Each time I called Gloria that month she said the same thing: "There's help for you here. Why don't you come on home?"

Home. She could say that her place was my home after all I had done, all I had put her through? It boggled my fried brain. "I'm not coming home," I told her. I had just called to check on them, to see if they needed anything, to be sure they were all right. Her new attitude had affected me already.

"There's help for you here," she repeated. "Why don't you come home?"

Home.

Gloria had begun attending Jim and Micah's church, Mid-Cities Bible, where Pastor Jim Shirling preached the meat of the Word and the congregation gathered her in. She drank it in as fast as she could and it made her a new woman. She was at peace with herself and with God. After all those years of searching, she had found a God of love and principle. The church prayed daily for B. J. He didn't know why the drugs had little or no effect on him. He didn't know why he couldn't sleep. He didn't know anything. He was just restless and anxious and at the end of his rope. The people at Mid-Cities Bible Church prayed that he would have no peace until he came home, home where he belonged.

I couldn't fight it much longer. I thought if I could just get next to Gloria I could draw some strength and maybe get some rest. I was doing nothing, yet I was exhausted and unable to sleep. On January 24 I called her again.

"Hello, Gloria; this is me. How's everything?"

"Everything's fine here, B., it really is. How are you?"

"Well, why is everything fine, Gloria? What's happened?"

"I'm different, B."

"How are you different?"

"Well, I did something, but I'm not going to tell you over the phone. You come home. There's help for you here."

Home. She was accepting me in spite of myself. That wasn't Gloria. The divorce papers were just days from completion, yet she wanted me home.

"ok," I said, "I'll come home for a few days."

I didn't know what else to do. Maybe I could relax there and get some sleep. I was afraid of getting any more hard drugs because I would rather have been dead than crazy. And the coke had made me crazy. If there was help at home, I didn't care what it was. It was worth a try.

Gloria didn't tell Paige, who had just turned six, that her daddy was coming home. There had been too many false alarms, and Gloria couldn't count on B. J. until he got off the plane.

On the morning he was supposed to arrive, January 25, Paige told her mother a story of something that happened at school. "I put in a prayer request about my dog," she

*said. The dog had never taken to her and didn't seem to like
her. The kids had prayed that this would change. As she
told her mother the story, the dog scampered to Paige and
teased. She didn't even act surprised. Her faith had been
confirmed.*

"I put in another request too, Mommy."

"And what was that, honey?"

*"That my daddy will come home. I know he's going to
come."*

*Gloria bit her lip. She wished she could be as sure. A
few minutes after Paige left for school, B. J. called to say
he wasn't coming.*

I woke up sick. My body was in agony. I was vomiting and
miserable. "I'm not going to be able to make it," I told her.

"You do what you have to do," she said. "But Paige thinks
you're coming."

I told the guys I'd be back in a few days, took my drugs
with me, and barely made the plane. I felt better once we
were in the air, but I didn't know what to expect at home.

A cordial, guarded Gloria met me at the airport. She
was alone. On the way home I asked, "Now what is all
this you've been talking about?"

"There's no way to tell you but straight out," she said.
"I've become a Christian and have turned my life over to
Jesus Christ. He is the answer to why I am different."

I'd heard it a million times before—not a few times from
Gloria herself—but this was different. This "turning your
life over" business was a whole new ballgame. It sounded

so real, so personal, so concrete. Not the abstract religious jargon I had been used to. I didn't tell Gloria, but it also sounded attractive to an otherwise hopeless drug addict. It was some idea—turning your whole life over to someone else. I sure hadn't done much with it on my own.

But I had other things on my mind, like getting some rest. Gloria didn't press the subject or badger me about smoking pot around the house. I had wondered how she would react to my still being an addict, but it didn't seem to make any difference to her. She was just loving me and accepting me the way I was. It was saying ten times more to me than words ever could have.

She wanted me to stay. "I'd really like to," I said. "I love you and I think I always have. But haven't I already destroyed us? Do I have a right to even think of coming back for good?" We'd been through it so many times before.

All the while I was thinking hard about staying, I was making a conscious effort to put off any confrontation with God, and especially with the Jim and Micah Gloria talked about. I was content to watch whatever it was work in Gloria's life. It sounded like a commitment far beyond my capabilities.

It meant a lot to me that Paige had prayed I would come home. I had never been anyone's answer to prayer before. And this was different than any kind of prayer I had been used to. This was really getting down to it with God and expecting him to answer specifically. Paige was excited to have me home and kept asking if I was going to stay. I told her that I was, but I really didn't know. I still had my stash

of dope and was doing some now and then. To look ahead
and see myself clean, living at home, worthy of the love of
my family? I couldn't.

I'd been home three days when Gloria said she needed
to stop by Jim and Micah's house. *Uh-oh,* I thought. *Here
it comes.* "Hey, let's only stay for a few minutes," I said. I
really didn't want to go. We got there about quarter after
seven, and the first thing I asked was, "What time does Jim
get home from the rodeo?"

"Oh, about ten-thirty or eleven," Micah said. I breathed
a sigh of relief. I figured I could squeeze out of there by
then. I didn't even balk at sitting down to a little dinner
with Gloria and Paige and Micah and her three children.
I had no idea the dinner would hook me.

It wasn't the food. It was the people. I just sat and stared.
Seeing these Christians with their glowing faces and pleas-
ant manner took me a million miles from the drug scene
and all the crazies I had associated with for so long—and
among whom I was king. They all looked bright and
happy, like they felt good. Suddenly I found myself anxious
for Jim to get home. I wasn't going to bail out after all.
Something inside was saying, "Look, you're here now. You
have been looking for an escape from drugs, and you'll
hear about the way out tonight."

It was too good to be true. I still doubted that I could
kick drugs, no matter what I heard, but I was desperate.
After all the roads I'd been down, my options were limited.

We waited and waited for Jim. I sensed God in that home
and I lost my fear. As the time dragged on, I became more

and more anxious to get to it. This wasn't like me at all. We didn't know that Jim had planned to work until midnight. At about ten-thirty he felt that he should go home. When he arrived, he realized why.

Here was this B. J. Thomas guy he'd been hearing about for so long. It was obvious that I made him nervous, though from the first minute I sensed his love for me. I told him right out that I wanted him to tell me about God.

Jim called a friend, Bobby Guess—a young guy who had been a musician and a drug pusher before becoming a Christian—to help talk with me. I think Jim felt inadequate, or maybe he had already sensed demonic activity and wanted support. The three of us sat around the dining room table, and they carefully talked with me and shared Scripture. The kids were sleeping and the wives were in another room, praying.

For the first few minutes I found my mind wandering. I wanted so badly to hear this, to get it down good, to know exactly what it was all about. But I couldn't concentrate. Why couldn't I set my mind straight just for a few minutes when I knew beyond all doubt that this was the most important conversation I'd ever had?

Jim saw something in my eyes that spooked him. I was with him one minute and not the next. It frustrated both of us. "Your eyes scare me," he said. "I see something looking back at me and it's not you." I didn't know what he was talking about, but I never doubted that evil forces were at work in me and had been for years. It's not hard to convince a drug addict of the reality of Satan.

"B. J.," Jim said, "I want to pause right quick here and pray, just in case any of Satan's forces are at work." I agreed. Whatever he thought was best was fine with me. "Lord," he prayed, "by the shed blood of Jesus Christ, I pray that if there are any demonic forces here, any wicked spirits, or anything of Satan interfering with B. J. hearing your gospel from the Word of God, you will make them leave."

Immediately I felt a disturbance in my chest and a sharp pain as if I had broken a rib. I sensed that something had left me. I was finally able to relax and a peace washed over me that I hadn't had for years. I enjoyed receptivity and clarity of thought so that every verse Jim and Bobby read just saturated me. I understood. I could just tell that God was about to do a work in me. It was almost impossible to believe that there might be genuine hope after all the years, the pills, the coke, the Valium, the hatred, the violence, the sin, the separation, the near-divorce.

Jim had no trouble establishing with me that I was a sinner and separated from God. I knew that full well. He said that it was important that I agree with God that I was a sinner. How could I argue? He read 1 John 1:9: "If we confess our sins, he is faithful and just to forgive us our sins, and to cleanse us from all unrighteouness."

The part of me that wanted to resist or put it off was already dead and I could hardly wait to confess my sins to God and be cleansed. There was more Scripture. Romans 10:9: ". . . if thou shalt confess with thy mouth the Lord Jesus, and shalt believe in thine heart that God hath raised him from the dead, thou shalt be saved." I knew it and had believed it most of my life. Could it be that now it was finally going to make a difference, that it was going to mean something personal to me?

Jim explained that I needed to ask Jesus Christ to forgive my sin, to save me and take over my life. He also emphasized that I needed to make Jesus Lord of my life and not just Savior. I knew exactly what he was talking about. Jesus just might have become my Savior when I was thirteen, but Christ had never become my Lord—that had been obvious. When Jim had shared with me all the pertinent Scripture, he encouraged me to decide what I was going to do with the information. "Just pray what's on your heart, B. J." I nearly shook with anticipation. I was more ready than I had ever been, but still I could hardly believe it was happening.

I began a twenty-minute prayer that was the most sincere thing I had ever done in my life. And I know the Holy Spirit authored it, because it was so precise and perfect that it couldn't have been the work of a scoundrel who had never prayed much more than "Thank you, God," before.

"Lord," I said, "yes, I am a sinner. I can see that right off. I know that I am undone. Without you, I can't make it. I believe that you sent your Son to die for me and that you would have done that for me even if I had been the only person on earth.

"Lord, I want you to come into my heart and make me new. It takes more faith than I've got, but I'm trusting you to do the work anyway."

Then I gave him myself. My drugs. "I can't beat it myself, so I'm just giving you the whole problem." There wasn't a doubt in my mind that he could handle it for me, though even that miraculous confidence amazed me. I knew from the minute I opened my mouth that I was talking to the living God, the Creator of the universe, and he was going to answer. It was a sweet conversation, not emotional, but to the point and covering all the bases.

I admitted everything I had ever done to my wife and child and other loved ones, and I asked him to forgive me and put it behind me. I had never talked with God this way, but I knew I had to go one step further, not for salvation, but for making my life different. I told the Lord that I wanted him to forgive me, too, for what I had done to myself in abusing my body and allowing myself to stray so far from his face. I wanted to live for him. There was no way I could do that on my own. I had no basis, no foundation. He would have to work through me.

I got straight with the Lord everything I could think of, and the bridge between ten years of hell and a right relationship with God was just twenty minutes—the most unforgettable twenty minutes of my life. When I looked up after saying amen, it was midnight, January 28, 1976. The memory of seeing that second hand sweep by the *12* will never leave me. When Satan tries to accuse me of being inconsistent and thus doubt my salvation, I just point back to that night, that time, that place, that prayer, and I rebuke him, reminding him that right then, God made me a new man.

11   withdrawal

I was so relieved and free I could have jumped through the roof. Jim and Bobby cried while I smiled so big it hurt. Micah and Gloria joined us and we just loved each other and praised God. "I don't cry well," Jim said, and he went to another room to be alone. God had saved *me*—who would believe it?

My only fear came on the way home that night when I decided to flush my drugs down the toilet. No more pills, no more pot, no more coke, and not even any more Valium.

I had no regrets, but I dreaded withdrawal. I'd been through that nightmare enough, and now it would be worse because I had never really recovered from my eleven-day binge, which had begun just one month before. Now I was quitting cold turkey. Every time I thought of the inevitable symptoms, I got a sinking feeling in the pit of my stomach. The shakes, the hot and cold flashes, vomiting, hallucinations, bad dreams, evil voices, and maybe even epileptic seizures. It was going to be one rough night, and I was scared.

I couldn't imagine ever doing any more drugs of any kind again, but I confess I wished I didn't have to face the next few days of horror. I asked the Lord to help me endure. It wasn't just the withdrawal either. With addictions to Valium, amphetamines, and cocaine, and at least a psychological addiction to marijuana, I also expected to go crazy. When you come out straight and dry from withdrawal—if you make it—you can be flaky for five months. I'm talking strictly bananas.

I feared the weirdo I might become, but I got rid of all the dope I owned and got ready for bed. I lay there for thirty minutes, feeling drowsier as time went on rather than thrashing fitfully for several hours as usual. I had been an insomniac for years, but sleeping during withdrawal was out of the question. The symptoms made me quiver just thinking about them, but that gradually subsided as I realized that I was falling asleep. Could it be? I forced my eyes open and stared at the wall, fully expecting my body to erupt any second. But my eyes grew heavy and I couldn't stifle a smile. By God (literally), I *was* falling asleep! And I did. Had there ever been a shred of doubt about God's involvement in my new life, that first night off drugs dispelled it forever.

The next day I felt clean and refreshed. Normally it takes days to clean the system, develop an appetite, clear the eyes, and feel normal. I was new, and there was never one withdrawal symptom or craving for dope. Gloria and I went to a Christian bookstore and bought me a copy of the *New American Standard Bible*. I love that Bible. I didn't understand much of it at first, but as we studied at Mid-Cities Bible and read more frequently at home, it began to come alive.

The couple of hundred people at Mid-Cities are fantastic. They didn't make a big deal over me; they just welcomed me in. We met with the Reeveses for Bible study, and the pastor spent a lot of time with us too. We were growing, getting grounded in the Word, and loving every minute of it.

Gloria had taken me back, not so much because she loved me, but because, based on scriptural principles, she felt it was what God wanted her to do. I came back to her, not so much because I loved her, but simply because I wanted to be with her. Everyday we tried to express *I love you* in different ways, and I believe the Lord honored that by rekindling our romance. The more we said it and lived it, the more it was true. We were in love again. The old hassles were gone. The difference in Gloria had brought about the difference in me—I really believe that.

She had been led to take me back no matter what I was or what I did. I could see that it was not just something she was going to try for a few days—not even Gloria could have dreamed up this scheme. She wasn't just talking this time; she meant it. It had to be for real. She was practicing a biblical principle that fewer and fewer people still believe today. I don't pretend to be an expert on either the Bible or marriage, but for us it works.

When you've decided to live for the Lord, he's the first thing on your mind when you get up every morning. That carried Gloria for the first few days I was back, before I became a Christian. She thanked the Lord for the way I was and didn't demand that he change me or that I change myself. She told the Lord that she was content to take me as I was, if that was what he wanted. That's when he began to work. She loved me without judging and my rotten life stared me in the face in contrast. It brought me to God.

The more I grew in the Lord, the more fences I wanted to mend. I hardly knew where to start, but I first called Don and Jerry. They both reacted enthusiastically, although I think Don was just patronizing me. He knows it's for real now—in fact, he lives for the Lord too—but back then I think he was just happy to hear about anything that might make me able to perform like my old self.

Jerry was genuinely thrilled, probably because before any of us, Jerry grew up. Before any of us, Jerry began to do things in moderation. Before any of us, Jerry became mature. I don't guess I could credit him with having been *the* stabilizing influence in my life, but certainly he was one of them. He had been worried about me for a long time and was afraid I was killing myself—which I had been, of course. But now he knew I meant business. I don't know if he or Don or anyone felt dead sure it would last; I had turned over so many new leaves I had worn out a couple of trees.

I called Chips right away too. It hadn't been that long since I had intended to kill him. "I really feel bad, Chips," I said. "I need your forgiveness." Of course, he had already forgiven me; that's the kind of a guy he is. But now it was really straight and I knew we'd eventually get back together on a project. I felt I needed to do my first album on my own after that, however. That way, when we got back together we'd be on more equal footing and I would have proven myself. Then we could really cut loose as peers—which we did.

Don worked quickly to get me some engagements, the first in February at The Embers Club in Waldorf, Maryland, where I had played many times. This time would be different. First, I got things straight with Don. We'd had it out once before when I had told him I knew what his New York buddies were up to. But now I assured him that I loved him and that I wanted him to be my manager. "The day you can't do the job, I'll fire you," I said. "I want you to know that I think you can do it. Don't lie to me. Don't beat around the bush. Just do it." And he's done it.

That first engagement after receiving Christ was like starting all over. No dope clouded my senses or dulled my memory. I read my Bible in my hotel room, and Don and

I talked about the Lord a lot. There was power and energy in my singing, my throat felt good, and I sang better than ever, according to friends. Of course, I couldn't sing in such a place without telling the crowd what had happened to me. My reason for singing and performing had a new dimension. It was an adventure and I never wanted it to end.

Best of all was knowing I would leave the show without facing a miserable, sleepless night chasing pills and highs, maybe beating up someone or smashing up hotel property. No, I would watch some television, read some Scripture, and get a good night's sleep. In the morning I would be hungry for a hot breakfast. I drank in all that my senses could enjoy again.

Scipture began to mean more and more to me. I had always thought that the Bible was full of exhortations intended to step on your toes, but that's not God's design—unless you need it, of course. What I needed was encouragement and advice, and I found it in everything I read. James 5:16 and 1 Corinthians 10:13 became two of my favorite verses: "Confess your faults one to another, and pray one for another, that ye may be healed. The effectual, fervent prayer of a righteous man availeth much"; and "There hath no temptation taken you but such as is common to man; but God is faithful, who will not permit you to be tempted above that ye are able, but will, with the temptation, also make the way to escape, that ye may be able to bear it."

That verse meant a lot to me, especially during my first year as a believer, because God proved it by not allowing one pusher to approach me the whole time. I think he knew that I wasn't ready for that kind of pressure and let me get grounded in his Word and with his people before allowing any tests. The tests came eventually, of course. Once in a Reno hotel I ran into a guy who was looking for the ice machine. I invited him into our suite since we had one. He appreciated it and said, "Before I leave, let me give you a little something." He pulled a vial of cocaine from his shirt pocket.

"No thanks, man; we don't need that," I said. I think old Satan wanted me to give that guy some ice, just because he had that coke.

Other verses that I've grown to appreciate especially are the ones in Ephesians 5 that talk about a man loving his wife as Christ loves the church. That's impossible, humanly speaking—loving your wife to the point of being willing to die for her, I mean—but through Christ, I can do all things (Phil. 4:13). I have claimed that promise and have attempted to follow the principle too.

I also enjoy reading and rereading John 3:16, "For God so loved the world, that he gave his only begotten Son, that whosoever believeth in him should not perish, but have everlasting life," because that *whosoever* was B. J. Thomas. It is still too good to be true.

My career became great fun again because I could appreciate all of it. I realized quickly that the Lord had protected me against singing any hit songs during the early years that I have to be ashamed of now as a Christian. Of course, they weren't Christian songs; they were frivolous, just for entertaining. But a lot of people loved them and enjoy hearing me sing them. And those songs have earned me the right to be heard.

My audiences have always been very receptive to hearing the gospel. Often I share just by saying that I don't want the evening to get too far along without giving a testimony for my Lord Jesus Christ. "And the best way I know to do that is to sing it." Then I sing "Without a Doubt" and "Home Where I Belong." Sad to say, I have found the secular audience much more receptive to a Christian witness than the Christian audience is to secular music.

There are days, while traveling and performing, that I find myself without time to read the Word as I should. I keep working at making time, because I know I need it, but the Lord has given me a short boost to keep me going when I need edification. It's no substitute for regular Bible study, but it sure gives me a spiritual shot in the arm. You know what I do?

12　home where I belong

I look in the mirror. I am my own best evidence.

I vividly remember the horror of life without Christ, and when I see myself reflected with clear eyes and a real smile, I know I'm a different person because of what God did. There was no way I could have done it myself. I had tried countless times. Only one in ten thousand junkies as far gone as I was ever live more than a few years, let alone kick drugs.

I still struggle with ego, temper, pride, and other personal traits, but God has protected me from falling back into drug-related or sexual sins that Satan could use to really devastate me. I run from all such temptation, and while Satan waits for me to let my guard down, he works on making me doubt my status with Christ. But I have my memory of that night, and I have the Word of God, and I have my transformed marriage, and I have a mirror that shows me a new man.

I recently had a couple of experiences that worked together to keep my attitude right. In fact, my attitude will probably be right for quite a while, just because of what happened. First, I was playing an engagement in Wilmington, Texas, and it was hot. Some of the people in the audience were old and they had to move toward the door for some air after a while. I was livid. I didn't say anything, but inside I was seething. *You don't walk out on* me, I thought. *Not on* me!

Then a week later I played a benefit for the Crippled Children's Home in Rosenberg, near where I went to high school. One of the kids was making some noise and I thought it was just somebody raising a ruckus. So I stopped and said, "Hey, man, you've got to be quiet. You've gotta shut up. Now shut up." The place grew deathly still and then I realized that it had been one of the *crippled* children!

I felt so small I could have fallen through the floor. "Hey, I didn't mean it," I said. "I'm sorry. You go ahead and have yourself a good time." But there was no taking back what

I had said or how I acted. I felt terrible, but it was a lesson I needed to learn, right there before a small audience of hometown people who would forgive me.

It's when you get tired of traveling and singing that you find yourself saying things on stage that you wish you hadn't. I have to quit traveling some day soon. This year we're taking Paige out of school and taking a tutor with us on the road so we can all be together, but someday this kind of life has to end. One day you wake up and find yourself thirty-six years old and sitting in the Holiday Inn in Minneapolis for the fourteenth time in your life and you have to wonder what it's all about.

I can't be perfect and it's futile to try to be. What I do try to be is surrendered. It's not easy and I fail often—too often. But I know where to go for healing and a new slate. I don't have to be shot down to ground level again every time I sin. I can get things right with God, ask his forgiveness and strength, and pick up where I left off. The dying to self and the growing are what it's all about. It's not the trying, it's the dying.

Jerry and I avoid temptation on the road by dealing creatively with boredom. It used to drive us crazy. We'd be on the thirtieth of forty-two consecutive one-night stands and the next day we'd follow the same routine—on the bus at 8:00 A.M., ride to Louisiana, get set up, get something to eat, sit around for several hours, take a shower, dress, do the show, go to bed, and then get up and do it all again. After a few weeks of that, all you want is some grass or a few hits of cocaine to make the bus seem a more mellow place.

But the Lord has put us onto a key antidote to that poison. We plan ahead to eat up the boredom with reading, watching TV, or just sitting and talking. We can be bored without going nuts. And if you're neither bored nor nuts, you don't need dope.

The road used to be horror—all highs and crashes, violence, sickness, defeat. Now it's as fun as it can be, especially when Gloria and Paige can come along. Everything is new and fun, and I am able to concentrate more on doing a good job and sharing Christ than on just trying to get on and off the stage in one piece and then go score some stuff. Those days were filled with fear of the next disaster, wondering what it would be and whether we could survive it. Now we look forward to every new morning, wondering what the Lord has in store for us that I would have been unable to appreciate before.

Johnny Cash's book *The Man in Black* meant a lot to me soon after I received the Lord, because his story is so similar to mine. I read most of it through moist eyes. I hope my professional life parallels Johnny's in some ways also. His success has given him many opportunities to speak out for the Lord. He has a unique sound and is respected in the business. People tell me that my sound is all my own, too, so maybe I'll turn the corner some day soon and become more well known and respected, not for my sake, but so I'll have a broader platform from which to share Christ.

When an executive of Word, Inc., a Waco-based Christian book and record company, heard me perform, he asked if I would consider cutting a gospel album with them. We recorded *Home Where I Belong* on the Myrrh label in November of 1976 and released it in 1977. I first gave my testimony in connection with its promotion at a Word reception for bookstore dealers and local media at the Universal City Hotel in Universal City, California. Not long after, I received a letter from a man whose daughter had joined him there and had taken home an album. I was glad to hear that she came to the Lord through listening to it, because not long after that she was killed in a car wreck.

Reaching people for Christ through records was something new to me, and it made the business successes pale in contrast, though they were impressive too. The album was the religious bestseller for over a year and was the first Christian recording to get a cover review in *Record World* magazine. It was number one on the gospel chart in *Cashbox* for about four months and won a Grammy award early in 1978.

When you're in the pop music business, it becomes second nature to sell records. That's what makes the career go, so we're not ashamed to admit that it's our main concern, other than ministry. I believe that it would be a great testimony for the Lord if the guy who had all but ruined his life and marriage came back to be a superstar because God had changed his life. The more records we sell, the more we can glorify the Lord. That's why it doesn't make me feel bad to say I want to be a big success in the business. Would the Lord want me to shoot for mediocrity? As long as he has called me to serve him in this field, I owe him my best effort. I know the commercial side turns off a lot of

Christians; sometimes it turns me off too. That's why I pray that we keep it in perspective and that we pledge to do all to the glory of God.

I believe the Lord withheld national fame from me— even during the years when I was selling millions and millions of records—because he knew I was not ready to handle it. I certainly wouldn't have glorified him with it then. Perhaps this time around he'll grant it so it can be used to further his kingdom. For ten years I had captive audiences and nothing to say. Now I have something to say and people learn quickly where I'm coming from and where I stand.

I wished I'd had something to say to Elvis Presley. When I get mad at the opportunists who are making money off his death and never once tried to help him when he was alive, I have to look at myself and admit that I didn't have anything to offer either. Never once did I sit down with him and say, "El, can we do something? Can we talk about your drug problem?" I know, it would have offended him, just like it would have offended me if someone had tried to talk to me—but it might have made some sort of an impact. No one did it, so we'll never know.

I was proud to be asked to sing at his memorial service in August of 1977, because I know he was a believer and I always admired him. I just wish I could have done or said something, but when I was close, I wasn't any better off than he was—and was probably worse off. One thing you could always say about Elvis was that he loved performing and he loved people.

I was so introverted when I began in the business that I couldn't even think about loving it. Now I'm more alive and in tune with the audience and I love the way it feels when it's being done just right—when everybody's cooking, from the light and sound guys to the band. You always leave the stage more pumped up than when you walked on, and you have to be pumped up when you walk on—at least I do.

A crowd that has heard my records is great fun to work with. I like to sing the same way in person as on the records. I try to give the soft pop sound a natural relaxed feeling, and I guess that's why my records always cross over and are good sellers on the pop and rock charts, as well as country. The greatest compliment a person could pay my music is to listen and sing along with it and think that he can sing just as good as me. He probably can't, of course, or he'd be in the business, but I want it to sound that way anyway.

Contemporary music can appear easy to sing, but really it's the toughest kind of vocalizing you can do. I mean, if you're going to record rock and roll, just get behind the microphone and rock and roll (that ought to get me in trouble with my rock friends!). But with the kind of music we try to sell, the combination of musician, vocalist, producer, tune, and lyric has to have just the right feeling. It's a challenge, especially when you're clear-headed and straight, and a Christian.

Since I've been a Christian, I've been pulled in every direction by the secular and the Christian world, and I've learned a few things. It's hard to give your testimony every night for two years. And it takes divine, intervening grace to put up with some of the things people demand in the name of the Lord. I have come to realize that the main thing the Lord would have me do is not to sing or perform or cut albums—even gospel albums—or give interviews or write books or even go on TV and talk about Christ. The main thing the Lord would have me do is live for him on a daily, personal basis. Whether or not I ever said so in public would not mean as much to him as my being sold out to him on the inside, at home, alone, when the chips are down and there is no audience.

As far as having anything heavy or spiritual or terribly pertinent to say, I confess that's not my long suit. I'm a country boy made good on the music scene, a drug addict saved by grace. I will glorify the Lord in any way I can in what I say and often in what I don't say. I'll share my testimony before secular crowds with gospel songs and I'll share Christ personally with fans after the show and with my friends and co-workers. I'm just a regular old middle-class dude who's better in a one-on-one situation, regardless what the rest of the Christian world thinks is required of a "star."

I can only do what God leads me to do, and I believe that is to stay in my profession and be myself. I'm not Johnny Youthleader or Joe Devotional. All I can be is B. J. Thomas, born-again pop singer. When you come to one of my concerts, that's what you'll hear, a B. J. Thomas show. You won't hear a sermon or a speech. You'll hear me praise

Jesus through my songs, because that's part of me. I can't count the number of times I wished people had understood this without my, or someone in my organization, having to explain it.

I played Las Vegas after I became a Christian, and was on the receiving end of a lot of criticism about it. I maintained that Jesus himself would minister there if he were on earth today. Some friends said to stay there and witness. Others said I shouldn't perform there. No one really swayed me until I got a letter from a group of Mennonites in the Tahoe area. I had not had a peace about playing Vegas, in spite of the fact that no one had talked me out of it, but their letter hit me between the eyes.

It said, in effect, that sure, Jesus went among sinners, but he didn't work for them. It was true. Unarguable. Jesus fellowshiped and dined with Matthew, but he didn't collect taxes with him. My mind was made up. I spoke with an evangelist friend who confirmed it. "If that's what the Lord is tellin' you to do, then do it. Don't procrastinate. If he wants you out of Vegas, get out."

I also told my friend that I was embarrassed and ashamed about my smoking. Many friends had said, "Don't worry about it. When the spirit is right, you'll quit." Well, the spirit never got right and Gloria and I both struggled with our habit. We knew that a God who had helped me kick a $3,000 a week drug habit could help me quit cigarettes, but still we hung on, nurturing our learned habit. It was the toughest thing to quit, but when my evangelist friend

looked me in the eye and said, "Yes, it's hurting your testimony and it'll kill you one day," I knew the time had
come.

I knew that if we knelt and prayed about my smoking,
I'd never touch another cigarette again. Here was a man
blessed and honored of God. A man who saw thousands
come to Christ through his ministry. I just knew that if he
agreed with God and me in prayer, it would be done in
heaven. And it was. By the end of the first quarter of 1978,
Gloria and I had quit smoking, cold turkey.

It wasn't easy. In fact it was one of the hardest things we
have ever done. I'd be hypocritical if I didn't admit that it
made me irritable and miserable and that I was hard to
live with for a month. Gloria and I fought more than we
ever had since we'd become Christians. It didn't bother her
as much because she has also gotten into health food and
has deleted sugar from her diet, but it was a rough period.

I still crave cigarettes from time to time, but the temptation alone pushes me closer to Christ because I know I can't
beat them on my own. I even am tempted to try dope now
and then, my mind telling me, *Drugs weren't so bad. It was
you. Boy, I'll bet you could handle them now*. No way.

When I get older, I hope I'll still be cutting records. But
more importantly, I hope I'll be just that much older in the
Lord. Every day I try to build new memories because the
old ones are painful. The first summer and winter I spent
as a Christian seemed like the first times I had ever really
seen the wonder of those seasons. I loved the beauty of the

snow, but the only memories I had of winter were of walking around New York City stoned or hanging around the fireplace in Connecticut smoking dope.

I've just recounted all of the old memories for you, at least the way I saw them through my clouded sensors, and I don't want to have to dredge them up again. It makes me emotional to think of the pain I inflicted, the months away from my wife and precious daughter. . . . You can see, I want to put all that behind me. If this book helps in any way, then I'll be glad I got it down on paper, but for now, I want to look ahead.

I'm into my third year as a Christian and I never realized how beautiful life could be. I have new resources and perspectives for dealing with the little irritations (and the big ones) that come along. It's a struggle, but it's a lot easier when you remember what we have to look forward to.

This old earth is really pretty to a mind that's been cleared by the power of God, but when we leave here, we'll *really* be home. Home where we belong.